*Zither*

*& Autobiography*

*Wesleyan Poetry*

# Zither

# &Autobiography

Leslie Scalapino

WESLEYAN UNIVERSITY PRESS

MIDDLETOWN, CONNECTICUT

Published by Wesleyan University Press, Middletown, CT 06459

© 2003 by Leslie Scalapino

Printed in the United States of America

5 4 3 2 1

Library of Congress Cataloging-in-Publication Data

Scalapino, Leslie.
  Zither & autobiography / Leslie Scalapino.
    p.  cm. — (Wesleyan poetry)
  ISBN 0-8195-6476-1 (cloth : alk. paper) — ISBN 0-8195-6477-x (pbk. :
alk. paper)
  I. Title: Zither and autobiography. II. Title. III. Series.
  PS3569.C25Z58 2003
  811'.54—dc21                                                  2003002730

# Contents

*Zither*

*& Autobiography*

Figure 1. On right: author, Leslie Scalapino, at age 7 or 8.
On far left: older sister Diane, author's mother, and
younger sister, Lynne. Photographer unknown.

# Autobiography

We assume that life *produces* the autobiography as an act produces its consequences, but can we not suggest, with equal justice, that the autobiographical project may itself produce and determine the life and that whatever the writer *does* is in fact governed by the technical demands of self-portraiture and thus determined, in all its aspects, by the resources of his medium? And since the mimesis here assumed to be operative is one mode of figuration among others, does the referent determine the figure, or is it the other way round: is the illusion of reference not a correlation of the structure of the figure, that is to say no longer clearly and simply a referent at all but something more akin to a fiction which then, however, in its own turn, acquires a degree of referential productivity? —PAUL DE MAN, *Rhetoric*, 69

Note: The names of people, where they are not otherwise described, refer to poets. Norman Fischer is a poet who at the time of my writing this was also the Abbott of the Zen Center at Green Gulch and San Francisco.

Two who aren't poets: This autobiography is dedicated to dear friends, with whom I hung out, Ruth Eisenberg and Joanne de Phillips. And is also for my beloved parents.

OCT. 14, 1997

Dear Norman,*

*Influence of Eastern Thought* on my writing—[that influence] 'thought' for me is entwined with early events / actions and geographical place: sense of utter freedom (my older sister and I riding all over Rangoon in rickshas—our parents away in northern Burma; our wandering walking

*Norman Fischer. This letter was the beginning of a collaborative exchange between Norman Fischer, Alan Davies, and myself on the subject of *Influence of Eastern Thought*; the exchange was solicited by Gil Ott, Singing Horse Press. It was later decided that we wouldn't use letters in the exchange; so far we haven't continued the exchange.

around Bombay by ourselves and going to Indian movies; my older sister and I staying, while our parents were away, in a missionary boarding house in northern Thailand, my reading while there about Buddhism (had visited temples in Japan), our bicycling by rice fields racing Thai girls)—in comparison with which coming home to Berkeley to school regimen at Willard Jr. High was torturous oppression which then made me want to do away with oneself.

The latter (initiating dying) was associated also with learning about death—(climbing over rows of sleeping people on the streets of Calcutta at 3 a.m. arriving there.—Seeing a man starving skeleton in a port lying in garbage; I was about seven or eight, walking in the garbage came up to him, my mother walking quite far ahead without looking back, a ship's mate with expression of concern coming up to accompany me glancing ahead after my mother—this only one incident, which I remember positionally, spatially)—reading about Buddhism there was no 'God' and we have to die. There is no authority anywhere or in one.

I freaked out and beginning then [at fourteen] sought (later in writing) the 'anarchist moment'—the moment that would be only disjunction itself.

In the process, I've created this memory track. Yet had the sense that I had to make fixed memories move as illusion, that they move as illusions.

Earlier, when I was seven, traveling with my family in Taiwan, I saw an old woman doing road labor as a "coolie" carrying heavy baskets of dirt; she had tiny bound feet and could barely hobble. I grasped then that only upper class women bound their feet as girls—i.e., her circumstance had disintegrated (I thought then seeing her, one must 'understand [or study] reality' (i.e., there is no choice) [I didn't have words for thoughts]—one must seek what would be called 'enlightenment,' but I hadn't heard such a word.

I can't sit [zazen] very well though I try, because my mind is conflict and active fantasy—partly because I write. It's almost seeking illusion, as if before event. (But this could also occur as sitting, is not alien to it—?)

For me, writing's experimentation of mind formation. One 'has to' leave formation, not be in formation.

I had the sense of being taken apart by having to return to a separated-culture (here—interior conflict as such: i.e., interior conflict is the exterior [as conceptual social framework], is oneself. One feels this as: separate as one. One feels it in movement anywhere). My writing is making interior illusion [making one's interior be illusion]—and is simultaneously also making the exterior, event and action as writing, illusion.

Leslie

OCT. 21, 1997

*In regard to laughing*—crossing lush, green Taiwan in a train car seated together, my younger and older sister and I were singing [I was seven]. Then I realized we were singing in public.

I was embarrassed; but looking around I perceived that my mother (sometimes looking encouragingly or contentedly at us, pleased that we were happy) and the other adults in eyesight all of whom were Chinese didn't think this was unusual. That children sang in public.

The train, traveling through one village after another by rice fields so incredibly green that it is imprinted later on the retina 'as if' memory, then stopped for a long time by one small village. My older sister and I ran forward through the train cars. A six-year-old girl had been killed, run over by the train. Her arms and legs had been cut off and were lying beside the track.

The entire village of adults stood by the embankment all in a line shaking as bending appearing to be laughing because the gesture of laughing and weeping were the same.

Later, knowing it was manner of 'extreme' emotion of crying, I asked my father They were laughing? He said No, it appears to be the same but they were expressing grief. I took note interiorly later also that they were demonstrating strong emotion for a little girl. This indicated a difference between what people said occurs at all [in society] and what occurs in fact.

On that same trip, traveling by freighter from port to port, the stevedores loading the cargo by hand and with cables under the lights and sound in hot nights the open hold of the ship, with the cargo loaded down swinging in—endless freedom of one place to another, a series [where there can be no conclusion or process even]—we were in I think Calcutta then, surrounded in the street wherever we walked by large numbers of beggars who would hold one hand out and with the other touch the belly and wail. At the time, there was a famine and draught; and disturbance [war] between Moslems and Hindus.

In Calcutta, my sisters and I sat with our grandmother [my father's mother, called "Mimi" by her grandchildren] in a horse-drawn cart outside a government building where our parents were inside dealing with a problem of visas.

They were in there a long time. A huge crowd of beggars gathered all holding out hands, touching their bellies, wailing and pushing the cart from all sides. One could not give money to any because there were too many. The suppressed force in the distance of the crowd was an incredible wave. The crowd occupied what seemed a vast location and surrounded us.

We crossed India in a third-class train compartment, in which leather benches were attached to the walls with iron-chain hinges and one looked out through barred windows.

The ground was desert with huge cracks, white cattle wandering in the sun. With no shade, shadow of skeleton trees. At every train station crowds of beggars occupied the platform, pursued the departing train with outstretched hands.

On one platform I began vomiting in the sun. My mother had me sit and she stood over me to cast a shadow.

Her futile gesture giving one young boy a sandwich and as we departed in the train we watched him open the bread as if looking for something recognizable to eat and, disappointed, throw the entire sandwich away.

On that platform my father bought a block of ice. We all took our shoes off and placed our bare feet on the block.

It was summer, boiling. Going to sleep only in our underpants at night, one's body sticking to the leather bench, one woke in a crowded train station, people packed into the car, one taking an entire bench having been asleep. Embarrassed at taking so much. The adults standing. Also not being dressed. No one minding. My father, mother, and grandmother jammed together seated nearby, their eyes closed asleep heads bobbing.

Later, [I] remarking with fear about ever returning to anything, any gesture repeated, as any repetition being conservative in one's life.

In Japan we saw Noh drama and Kabuki, masked gorgeous figures making cries, slowly moving stamping their feet—it went on for hours—

as a child I did not distinguish between being in the audience, the audience, and the dancing figures. One was surrounded [pleasurably] and in amongst [spatially] the sounds they were making.

I think crowds were the thing that needed to be traversed.

I saw *The Bald Soprano* [as a young adult], the unintelligible incessant exchange of non sequiturs by a lineup of parrot-people, words back and forth like badminton—seated my muscles became flaccid throughout my frame, my jaw fixed open in laughter which was unable to make a sound and I was not able to close the jaw; weak frame slipping liquidly from the chair, terrified I would fall to the floor in the midst of the audience who were also gaping. Weakly hitting one's hand against the shoulder of the man who was my husband then to ask for help but the hand was so weak he didn't notice. The response was laughing short-circuiting the brain so that it was in the muscles with no mind response, or it had closed down that passage.

My older sister and I [at thirteen] in Bombay went to see the movie *Mother India* with an Indian girlfriend around our age[s] who wept while the characters in the film encountered a series of catastrophes, famine, limbs amputated, flood, a mud slide sweeping the house away in which the figures sang, the woman sang wading waist-deep in mud. My sister and I burst laughing, our friend gazing at us in the dark shocked.

Later in Berkeley I went to see the three-part Cuban film, *Lucia*, presented by a socialist group; in the audience were all young adults as was I. Part one is a silent film, made in the silent era; a woman's lover woos her to run away with him, convincing her to take him to the place where her brother is hiding with the revolutionary army. The lover has set her up; when she takes him to her brother's hideout, the pair of lovers are overtaken by his collaborators, the counterrevolutionary army, who thunder past her and around her on horseback destroying the army of her allegiance and killing her brother. Her silent facial expressions, and movements whipped by the sides of horses going by, are impassioned Noh.

While I was transfixed by this part of the film, the young Berkeley audience roared with laughter, jeering loudly at the woman's facial expressions conveying motion, emotion which was ridiculous to them. It could not be seen as real.

In New York City at La Mama's Theater I saw a production in Greek of *The Trojan Women* in which the audience not having chairs roamed beside the actors; they were the crowd while a naked, head-shaven woman covered with mud and being jeered, is carried in a cart to her execution. Unknown language, one having the sense there is no language at all, so no known circumstance. Women jumped or fell, plummeting from burning walls, that were slides [not afire] from the walls surrounding us.

The walking audience was the crowd that perpetrated or participated in/saw these events—in the space, against one's 'will.' I freaked out, losing it inside, frightened I would begin to weep, be in public and come apart.

In the same area of the walking audience, three elderly audience members kept pace, padding in their sneakers, alertly clear-eyed and making strange comments in New York sound-dialect to the air like "Do you know a lot about Greek history?" Utterly compatible with me constricted near weeping in their location beside them.

Later visiting with Alice Notley, she asked what I thought of the performance which she also had seen. Describing it, from speaking the situation, [shortly after] I wrote an interior-play within a poem-play, called *leg*, rendering that speaking-interior.

Events in memory occur in the same time, are the same time. Having a hard time making a living, once I'd had to stay up without any sleep for two nights to finish an indexing job by the time it was due. Then I couldn't sleep, propelled without words or thoughts, with an inner agitation so extreme that I went out for a walk in the evening to try to be calm.

At the corner of College and Ashby in Berkeley, couples were crossing the street strolling blissfully arm-in-arm gazing at me benignly, beaming. I walked past them—their strolling—my caught up in an intense physical isolation, akin to busting up/one that is only its location.

But it is desertion—not by them.

[*Nov. 1, 1997*: Once, Alice peered at me (across a table at a café in New York City) I had been in rage outside of myself walking in the streets—had come in to speak to her—when she peered.

In *leg*, women jumping, dying, the men dead already, killed, in a brief action are superimposed as space/time on a taxi trying to pick one up because one must look like someone who would want, or needs, or would take, a taxi. Yet the former's occurrences are the interior of the one setting.

                    making jokes
                    out
                    - not in that

view
though it is

Traveling in New York City studying it as *structures* of events in writing. First conversations with Charles Bernstein, who among other thoughts and subjects introduced me to Robert Wilson's work *Einstein on the Beach* which I later saw; I also saw a three-hour production of Wilson's *The Civil Wars*. Charles and Susan Bee introduced me to the Hudson River School of painting, which gave me an idea beginning, or occurring early in, *The Return of Painting*. I was also influenced earlier by seeing many Japanese samurai movies, like Kurasawa's *Ran;* or *Harakiri, The Ballad of Narayama,* and *Ugetsu.*

[*Nov. 14, 1997:* I was of course reading constantly; in addition to the works of most of the contemporary poets, I had read as background Stein, Virginia Woolf, H.D., Proust, Shakespeare, 17th and 18th century English, French, and Japanese novels, picaresque structures, etc.]

In New York I went to see Pina Bausch, Meredith Monk, Carol Armantage, Laura Dean. Seeing dance and painting, or film, has been the most pervasive influence for me, as if the differentiation from text was necessary for writing. So—taking photos (*Crowd and not evening or light*) in Venice Beach and Waikiki, I wrote on them, or beside or below the photos, a line or several lines as unrelated place in space.

—

Earliest memory: walking to school [age four] falling on the ice always at the same spot where the dog barked [as soon as it barked, I fell], being coaxed by my older sister to try to walk across the ice—before falling. Her looking sympathetically at me as I fall—and before falling.

This early memory is coexistent with being taken to visit Mrs. Booderling (Cambridge or Boston, Mass.), an elderly Russian lady who knelt talking to me, playing. I was fascinated because my mother had told me Mrs. Booderling had fled Russia after the Revolution, trying to get to the border walking out with her husband and son. They were separated from each other in the crowds of walking people. Wandering into a village, she saw her husband and son shot in front of a firing squad.

My sense was, not fear but rather, that this is what it is to be an adult [to see such]—[*Oct. 22, 1997:* and that (seeing death of husband and son) a part of oneself as one's imperman[ence then].

Figure 2. Author, Leslie Scalapino, at age 2. Photo by Robert Scalapino.

I was born in Santa Barbara, California, but my earliest memories are of Boston or Cambridge, Mass. Being bathed with my older sister, Diane, in an iron wash tub by my mother, the water heated on a stove. We lived in a tenement building surrounded by tenement buildings, vacant lots in rubble where we played.

The playmates I remember were Bo-Bo who was three, and his older brother, Caucasians born in China. Bo-Bo spoke only Chinese, his brother translating helping him in a sympathetic way; but Bo-Bo would react with rage when he couldn't be understood. Standing in a rubble-filled lot, he threw a brick at us.

I went to kindergarten, though I was under-age. There wasn't a nursery school available. The other children, it was later described to me, were Irish. One girl brought fat to eat for lunch.

My earliest memory of my father was of him lying in bed at home, being given a treatment by a nurse who visited each day. He had contracted polio by swimming in the Charles River.* There was an epidemic. Having his muscles worked by the nurse. I stood watching at the foot of the bed where he lay; he gave an encouraging expression to

---

*After writing this I learned from my parents that he "never swam in the Charles River." I'm here retaining accounts, which in childhood I thought were facts, told by someone in the family.

Figure 3. Author Leslie Scalapino as an infant
held by mother beside older sister Diane.

include me, to indicate it was not serious. [His left leg and perhaps left side were paralyzed but recovered.]

My father was raised in Santa Barbara, California. His father (whose parents were farmers, my great-grandfather called by my grandmother Mimi a "feminist" and a "radical" as if to be such were glorious—the great-grandfather also described proudly by her as having been defiantly excommunicated from the Catholic Church (she may have exaggerated this)—sent five of their eight children to college, including three daughters sent to college in the early 20th century (?); my grandfather, Anthony Scalapino, studied theology and knew Hebrew? Greek, Italian, and English) was a high school principal; my father's mother a school teacher. My grandfather's mother, though she herself spoke with a strong accent, taught my father to read before he entered kindergarten. My father's father died right before I was born.

Once, when I presented my first book to my parents, my sitting at their house visiting with them, my father blurted "I read a hundred books in my first year of school and received a prize at the end of the year." My mother looked at my father and said, "Bob, it's not your turn." Both of my parents have a wonderful sense of humor.

Without financial resources from his family, my father who'd skipped two grades and taught at Santa Barbara College when he was twenty-one, studied at Harvard in Japanese/Chinese studies, becoming a political scientist who returned to California to teach at the University of California at Berkeley.

My mother, raised in Los Angeles, was a singer and musician. She was from a poor family, her parents divorced, her father worked for the Santa Fe Railroad. She was required early-on by her mother to wait on her three brothers. She was the first in her family to go to college, told initially by her parents that there was no reason to educate a woman. She had to begin to put herself through school, later receiving some help from her father. She attended Santa Barbara College, then the New England Conservatory of Music. She graduated from the University of Colorado at Boulder where my father attended Japanese language training to enter the navy on loan to the army in World War II.

He returned to Harvard after the war. He first became interested in Asia when, realizing he was going to be drafted, he chose to study Japanese. Later honored (as a political scientist/historian) as a "Sacred Treasure of Japan," he studied in officer language training at Boulder with other students such as Seidensticker and Donald Keene later scholars and translators of Japanese literature.

My father became a lieutenant [*Oct. 22, 1997:* a Japanese language officer, and was sent to Guam, Okinawa, the Philippines, then Occupied Japan; he read maps, translated, studied Japanese during his duty. I asked him once "What did you do in World War II?" He said "Nothing. I was supposedly being trained to be in the vanguard to invade Japan." [Assigned to search, after battles in Okinawa, for documents left or buried in caves—where Japanese soldiers were frequently still hiding—he once encountered an Okinawan man with his small son, the man holding a grenade. My father forgot all of his Japanese. But the Nisei soldier who accompanied him spoke eloquently, and the Okinawan man didn't use the grenade.] He told only a few stories: rounding up civilians on

Figure 4. Robert A. Scalapino, author's father.

Okinawa, putting them in trucks to get them away from the areas that were under fire—a young woman breaking away in fear and disoriented running toward the firing up a hill, at the crest of which was the firing; he ordered a marine to run after her and catch her. He said "I thought then: I've ordered him to do this, he may be killed." The marine caught her at the crest of the hill and carried her struggling back to the truck.

[He prepared leaflets to be dropped from planes telling civilians and soldiers they would not be killed or harmed if they surrendered, but he said sometimes the marines killed them.]

We went to the Philippines (I was thirteen). We were met at the Manila airport, a hot evening, by members of the family with whom we stayed there; whom my father had first met when, their family starving, they'd come to the army camp begging for food. They took us for a fast drive I think straight from the airport, to cool us in the heat conversing driving fast through an immense war burial ground for miles curving on the road in wind in which the gravestones shone in the dark. They took us in Manila itself to a shell that was a ruined cathedral, retained as a war memorial, in which two thousand Philippine civilians had collected for protection, and were fire-bombed by the Japanese soldiers.]

OCT. 22, 1997

*"Traveling is sentimental"*—Lyn Hejinian says to me as exchange in our collaboration, *SIGHT* (that is passages on seeing, 'poems'/'letters' ?, signed with our initials to distinguish the source, as speaking to each other).

Her phrase I think indicates 'travel' as memory and account or 'personal account' (as outside oneself, formed as description of oneself defined as 'traveler,' considered as pre-fab nostalgia, or stance which is fixed conception of oneself; as opposed to 'not knowing what one is' at any time in the writing)—rather than the phrase meaning travel as movement per se. Memory per se—as phenomena. Which one is examining in writing.

The notion that one's experience is 'clouding' occurrence makes sense. So does the notion that experience is exactly 'that' occurrence only as *being* one's impermanence.

My sense of 'traveling' is only motions—in a real infinite space and time that is anyone, as it is exterior *at once*.

One has to depart from both one's motions-in-events, from events, and from one's mind motions which are separate present—(which one does anyway) traveling continuous: in order to 'cause' that separation, as if motion 'before.'

So that one is in motions—before 'them.' Cognizance and motion overlap, and are the same. While being the same occurrence, in the same instant they occur separately.

('Here'—in the United States) where memory is associated with 'one' it's "subjective" and regarded negatively. Then "thought" is an academic 'field' (if it *is* that 'field,' it is categorical), it describes phenomena via its own categories only.

As writing memory per se present would have to be the interior of actions.

If we have to die—and given the pain that is ahead as having to live per se—hordes of beggars because it's occurring is inescapable—then we can see into others. i.e., This occurs. I was sitting on the sidelines of the baseball mound (age fourteen) on the ground with others [I'd freaked out, was a loon, then] and could simply 'see into' the other girls there, a few standing, simply hear or know what they were thinking specifically. One leaving oneself.

The capacity only occurred for a short time (about a year, maybe a few months—or weeks).

The capacity is extremity per se, just only that—yet itself not felt as extremity at all. Then in that particular situation, the teacher asked us to come up to play baseball and I refused to; the other students saying "If she doesn't have to, we won't either" so I got up, and went to the baseball mound. The teacher wasn't requiring me, bypassing or letting me off (because it's been noted I'm caught in interior gyrations in incredible pain in the midst of a class, unrelated-separated, clenching my fists to stop the tears which poured down my face while sitting at the desk—I wasn't clenched because the tears are public but because the fist-exterior and the being torn apart inside so continually were the same.

The algebra teacher said gently to come here and began, after the class had left, bending beside my desk, to show me the algebra problem—without his addressing emotion, his indicating how to center my attention).

My father also, while addressing the problem directly, did not approach it by addressing emotion itself as that isn't anything; although acknowledging my emotion, he apprehended the central issue. Frequently he came into my room to sit and talk—I was constantly in a violent hair-pin formation that's a motion as interior. He said "You are obsessed with death. At your age this is not necessary," meaning I have time to live (I was surprised he knew I was obsessed with death, that he could know that. His acknowledgment that no one will escape is no consolation—i.e. he was not lying).

[*Oct. 30, 1997:* He had (has) keen attention, directness of apprehension grasping something as a whole before it is spoken, or without it ever being spoken.]

At this time I found relief in reading Greek tragedies, first memorizing many of the myths and events, then beginning to read the tragedies. The unavoidability of the fate which the protagonist encountered—and that he was entirely fallible, that he had 'caused' it, which is outside him separate from his volition—the two were the same, is what seemed real to me. Similar to not possible to know anything. Emotion the accurate sole expression and completely delusory. Seen to be delusory while one is that.

Therefore the desire ever 'to return' is gone—in the place that is it—in that the predilection itself (of 'traveling') is relentless because an event. There isn't authority in 'event' or 'one.'

This degree of freedom at that age was 'impossible' for me.

I experienced continual vicious attack on myself from myself—as one being nothing ever—until finally I had a dream of a huge dog tracking me as I fled through vacant buildings, it continually reappearing stalking to kill me, then cornering me, at which I woke realizing the dog was myself, that I was going after myself and that my mind was taking care of me, telling me to stop doing this, while *being* myself. Amazed in seeing the mind is phenomena, and that it cares for oneself as if lovingly.

I read a sentence that the Greeks had the sense that people were their expression in society only, one had no existence if by or in oneself. I thought in that case I will be nothing because I am 'one' (my nature being introverted). Not: that is because *society* is nothing—as isn't the same as dying and as no-authority-ever.

I checked the San Francisco Chronicle for the arrivals and departures of freighters and their destinations to Asia, desperately wanting to stowaway.

But this is not 'experience.' [*Oct. 23, 1997*: Before traveling anywhere—something occurred (maybe age six). My mother put us to bed to sleep before waking us at midnight to go to the airport to meet our father.

I woke having dressed myself and tying my shoe crying. My older sister looking at me.

I woke having fully dressed myself—I thought why am I crying? and stopped crying. The impression I got is that we are not 'oneself' that isn't there. As if an instrument playing two or several notes at the same time.

What's mixed in with freaking out later—is their dividing the kids racially, their being abused, and one being helpless.

One math teacher baiting and insulting the Black kids (such as a girl with a note for having been sick, he accuses her of having been "shacked up with some man," shrieks you were shacked up with some man—and she trembles denying it) then imploring them "I need this job" to which they would respond with sensitivity/sympathy, only shouting and stamping their feet in response to separate occurrence, at a different time from being racially insulted or requested for sympathy.

The response would be displaced from the origin, slightly.

A girl asked to go to the toilet—I was called up to the desk in front of the class after she left instructed to follow her and look under the stall to see if she's there.

I think I looked under the stall, maybe not. It wasn't held against me by the others because we were being manipulated and oppressed.

He gave bad grades automatically, one mother seen by me in the hall begging him meekly not to give her child a D while he refusing even to speak to the woman.

(These are few isolated episodes.) Anger, emotion, was not 'felt' then or delineated—rather, it was outside; which is not of those actions. Though something's occurring.

As writing—there are (mental projection of) two horizon lines that are occurring at once superimposed spatially. The horizon's are 'one.' One's-impermanent ("one's-impermanent" itself is the particular situation delineated).

I wrote this language-shape in *that they were at the beach*.

(I would stop eating, managing to whisk the food off my plate and conceal it in a napkin in my lap, going for as long as a week without any food passing my lips. Parents out one evening, I swallowed sleeping pills bought at a drug store deciding to die but becoming frightened told my older sister, was taken to the hospital where my stomach was pumped, a tube run down my throat.) At dusk in cold autumn then walking beside the stream of pouring cars on Ashby Avenue trying to have the nerve to step out in front of them, eyes of the adults in the cars darting alerted, puzzled.

In that instance of that math teacher, my mother went to the principal. That math teacher was fired at the end of the year and the principal was demoted, made a math teacher.

Prior, one math teacher at Willard Jr. High made me pull on her hair to show me it was real after the kids had baited her for her red hair, their stamping and screaming. She was elderly, weak. Becoming senile. Sent kids to the office to get the principal the kids returning defiantly without him.

Then she died, after she'd wavered in the halls, and no one came to her funeral except one parent: we were crossing the Pacific on a freighter then—this hair pulling was 'before' one freaking out.]

*Approaching—walking on the deck.*

'First ocean'—[age seven]. We floated up in still ocean to black islands that were sunk deep in the water but floating on top of it—unpopulated small isles floating 'before' Taiwan.

Before that there was being in the typhoon on the ocean—walls so that the ship would dip entirely on one side almost touching the water with a wall of water over it.

My father, who had a cabin in the ship with his books where he worked, or that may be where my mother and he slept also, lunged through the hall all night to see how we were doing in our bunks.

I opened the heavy metal door to the deck by myself and saw the wall of ocean about to come down—barely closing the door.

We stayed in a hotel over a shaking railroad station—my older sister and I slept on an air mattress which deflated on the floor where cockroaches the size of an adult's palm walked on us. My sister said they did, I didn't see them.

We took turns trading crouching on a straight-back chair and sleeping with our bottoms in a small basin sink until dawn.

Then my mother rose without speaking indicating get on the bed; she lay down on the flat air mattress and continued sleeping where the cockroaches were.

We stayed in a hotel where many men and women ("coolies") carrying heavy baskets of dirt on poles on their shoulders were carving out a swimming pool.

On the curving hotel stair my mother scolded my younger sister who was three for a non-deferential manner of speaking to a servant of other Western children there, from whom my sister'd just heard this manner of speaking.

In a rage for being scolded at all, Lynnie stamped and wept in one place on the stair.

"Never, never speak in that way. To anyone. Ever again." What way? This had a strong effect on me.

In the mountains, in Japan, riding the bicycles through the pouring rain, lightning flashing around—ahead, the rear tire of the bicycle swayed with my younger sister seated on it wailing; screaming on the tail of the bicycle, another lightning flash coming down.

My older sister and I pedaling fast calling back and forth to each other skidding in lightning.

Hopping in potato or rice bags tied at our waist at night racing on a field with others—the fireflies and explosions of fireworks opening in the blackness.

Living with a Japanese family in Tokyo and in the mountains with them in summer. A bucket in the kitchen with eels.

Walking with Mimi who was teaching us the parts of the flowers.

In Tokyo being taught by Mimi and couldn't go out to play with our Japanese playmates until finished so looking from the window at my older sister jumping rope.

Snow—potato cakes cooked in a cart on the street.

My load too heavy and I couldn't carry it—my father took off jetting at a run to the railroad station leaving me behind.

Unwilling to leave my load in the street, I stood weeping. A tiny elderly Japanese woman who was my height carrying a huge bundle on her back tied with a sash coming on the road. She carried my package—my tears drying as I walked beside her—to the railroad station and looking around finds him.

In elegant Japanese he thanks her—and the tiny person chews him out.

Mimi reading to us. Mimi dancing the hula each night in her corset when we're lying on the tatami on our bed so we will laugh and then go to sleep. Blackness, when outside.

'One can't write narrative because people will not be able to distinguish it from what is occurring.'

Mimi holding an unlighted cheroot in her mouth by the ship's railing, by Rangoon, wrapped in a Burmese sarong. In her seventies.

A Japanese whaler on the Pacific, whales harpooned float all around us. A stowaway hidden in a box on the bridge of our freighter came out—and was sent in front of us in a row boat to the whaler. One of the oarsmen from the whaler on the choppy waves falls in—he's embarrassed—the stowaway waves.

One repeats things in the same place [dismantling it, by writing it, from actually occurring—from having actually occurred, and re-seen].

Jumping rope at home.

[These are almost the only memories I've got. An aspect of Zen practice is for the individual to undercut (highlight?), itself a conception, conception of their self so continually as to dismember their fixed relation to events, even while in the present of those events. Memory itself being only a construction (of itself), of the present also.

Figure 5.

I was using this process of dismemberment of one's own thought as
the instant of tackling the 'process of hierarchical definition' (to place
outside to remove from what it is), in U.S. culture 'what thought is in-
trinsically.' Without at an earlier time knowing about Zen logic or prac-
tice, I used in writing a mode of dismantling one's own thought that
may be similar to it.

In Japan, I had the sense of 'returning to oneself,' my nature inher-
ently calm not disrupted by impinging violence. Later, I had a logic of
dis-placement by which I lived as writing.* From *Orchid Jetsam* (which I
wrote under a fictional author's name, Dee Goda):

*Note on Orientalism: the places, the texts. Indian, Japanese, Tibetan, Chinese. My
orientation is respect for these texts and traditions, and a concerted effort to try to learn
from them. Such a view also informs my sense of reality that is political. For example,

"As 'their culture' and 'one's' are rendered at once the same through or as one interiorly, that one is that other (early), yet not known by it or accepted. Returning to one's own culture, one is outside, other than it—therefore 'it' critiques oneself (by oneself).

"Oneself cannot be anywhere.

"And one's own culture can be opened there . . .

"Then what is interior, defined by them. as other to them, is other only. Continually occurs as that.

"the relativity *is* that instant of one's only (intersects as joy)."

The syntax of writing, a thought-shape, is to be attention itself, the instant of reading or (as) being that thought-shape only. Attention ('shape'), even at that instant is only imitation of itself, changes (and changes oneself). I had the urgent sense that writing has to unpeel all constructions of action and perception in the instant of their occurrences in order for one to 'be' at all.

Even discursive intervention—seemed to me to be 'authority' replacing mind phenomena, both unseen. One has to do both.

(I thought intellect is *also* within, constructed, blind.)

Emotion is one's being in any instant—it seems to be—it moves with force, then is outside, a state through which one has passed. A thought is a similar state, unknown to one, not more stable. Thus to be within (the act of) constructing doctrine (either emotionalism or rationalism) as one's basis is delusory 'authority'—just as is being in the appearance of sequence of events, or one being in or reconstructing passionate emotion. Coming here (this culture), it *is* foreign. There wasn't any that's one's own.

---

after travel[[ing in Mongolia, I described to a friend the impact of Russian Stalinists on Mongolia—that they destroyed the Buddhist temples and monasteries, lined up many thousands of monks and executed them. The populace protected the temples, the statues and paintings within, by filling the interiors with grain, maintaining to the Stalinist activists that these "were grain storages. My friend, poet and critic, apparently Stalinist(?)-leftist, tight-lipped responds "I thought the Stalinists solved the problem of Buddhism (eliminated Buddhism)"—meaning, they should die. I believe that the sense of leftist political philosophy is akin to radical Buddhist philosophy. As Mahayana Buddhism's traditional, cultural manifestations, its practice (when it was practiced) was also nonviolent and conceptually liberating. This man's statement means: one group wiping out another with obtuse cruelty.

I had a sense there could be a different space (attempting this in my text, *R-hu*), for example, a 'coming into the same space' of Mongolian conceptual/ geographical space (their comparison of simultaneous plateaus in tankas—that are wall-size paintings—to their real outside, vast horizon landscape, the mind compared to it and to U.S. space). It's the sense of real place as a 'new' conceptual/ as geographical space [of writing now.

One person criticized *that they were at the beach—aeolotropic series* as nostalgia; yet I was trying to 'punch out' of occurrence real-time events at all, even literally holes.

Seeking to 'free oneself from memory,' knowing only those events that change one?

Not form oneself; also not form one's (U.S.) conventional apprehension, not a rendering or description of foreign place or perspective, isn't exotic. This notion itself is *apparently* (that is, overtly) subjectivity and illusion—the intention is to transform one's illusion of entity by being illusion.

Memory of lying face-forward on the futon in the dark in the mountains of Japan (age seven) and fearfully hearing the scratching of an insect, then hearing it was my own eyelashes on the pillow. A memory is an implant, like the memories placed mechanically in the Replicants in *Blade Runner*; it is all that one has.

The two 'implants' (memory and real) are opposites, both as if *exterior*—yet 'as' one's only modes of cognition. 'The two at once' '*being* one's mind' sometimes precipitated circuit-breaking so that something else happens—a leap outside of myself in the writing, that *is* the writing.

The mind itself being only allusion: conceiving of a writing that is without allusion at all (that it does not refer at all, is not 'in' memory), even any formed by repeated sound or resonance to hang onto, without plot on which to rely, was the implied project (impossibility, as being outside of language even).

The mind without allusion (allusion is the mind's inherent nature, as it is language), *arrived at as writing—as* an impossibility even—is 'directly' proposal of 'being outside what the mind can do, dropping the mind.' Dropping interior barrier (which is allusion also).

'Objectivity' *is* allusion always. My sense of language is to cross the line, or barrier, of its distinction. *So that* one is not in an ordered 'place' from which to perceive. Place as theory is thought-shape; written, it is language-space.

Separation of 'oneself as memory of hearing one's eyelashes on the pillow' from those events which are 'important events' or 'exterior events' in time (in the world)—necessarily, entails a predetermination as a hierarchy itself *that is* 'exterior events.'

This is related to—waking at night as young adult terrified one was not living *then*—living not being possible even if/while outracing oneself and events.]

*Not speaking*—both: until ready; and, not speaking at all at the time.

I went to John Muir elementary school in which the teachers chose favorites and excluded and spoke meanly to, regarded negatively, the children who were not the favorites.

The standard as 'pet' (as if 'at all,' in existence) being based upon sense of convention, personalities being this, before we know what this is.

Or those who were favored already behaved in a way that is convention.

At that age (nine or so), my friend in school spoke once about the situation, which amazed me—that it was seen by others and that it could be articulated.

Before her articulating the situation, I stopped speaking (to the teachers and principal—perhaps not speaking in school for the most part for as long as I was there; continuing to jump rope, play hopscotch, participate-as-watching).

The principal had me sent (age six or so) to her office where she asked me, both of us seated in large leather chairs, her across from me at a large mahogany desk, what I was thinking.

She said while I sat listening that I never spoke, "This is all right; but we just want to know what you're thinking?"

I didn't say a word throughout the interview. I think this was like listening to music, having to study it, throughout it, before hearing it. Then she said I could leave.

This is before traveling. Was at the same time as waking up having dressed oneself, and waking while tying one's shoe crying. The two are separate.

I was sent home once from school with a note pinned on my dress on my chest which read, "Won't speak." At the time I was happy or at any rate fine. I later felt a sense of great relief—when we went to Japan—as if the pressure had been removed from me and I could be.

(Lyn Hejinian who'd been a pupil there remembers this same principal earlier, a tiny, compact woman wearing a suit—who'd persecuted Lyn's younger brother so their parents had taken him out of the school. The first time I talked to Lyn she was giving me a ride home from a reading, at a time when she was writing *My Life*. We passed John Muir, her remarking she'd attended school there saying "I was teacher's pet." It was very funny.)

Seated alphabetically, I sat always amongst a group of boys who seemingly didn't respond to repression, would forget, be noisy and playful; for which they were always in trouble while I was in trouble because I was quiet.

These boys were my models for 'people'—also for 'men' (the impression being generosity, accepting of one for who one is).

[*Oct. 28, 1997:* Also, that 'people' were that 'only'—that they allow 'one to be oneself.'] All older people meeting me said that I was my father. I thought I was him only. That is, literally exactly him, there was not 'myself.'

One's a woman—one's father—. His being a double and a man—one being the same—dismantles separation. Between anyone. Dismantles any custom. Of sexism or any. So—then—how can friends betray one? That was/is later a real confusion.

I had a best friend who articulated the situation in school (critical of the teachers' authority, aware of it as convention), quite a ways into its effect, tonally mirroring *them*—not including me in the mirror which would have been speaking about or to me rather than as if she were aware 'objectively' of it. I had a second friend too.

The first had apprehended the entire situation while the two of us stood on the second floor looking down out of a window watching everyone playing on the playground, clusters of people here and there.

My mother waited at the back door to welcome me when I returned from school each afternoon; glad, indicating arrival was wonderful.

The professors who were my father's colleagues, all of whom described themselves as radicals and who tended to assess other's intelligence (as analyzing someone's "I.Q." assessing as "brilliant," a man who would be "great," or a man who was "mediocre"; mocking emotion or a viewpoint being emotional) would make comments assuming men's superiority in relation to women.

They would ridicule in tone, humiliate their wives at the dinner table to which the wives would say nothing, embarrassed. The women would think they were inferior?

Always it was the Western men who behaved in this way; these scenes were imprinted caustically in their present and later. For me, the scenes simply 'had occurrence' without comment from me to myself then.

My father didn't make ridiculing comments about women [*Oct. 29, 1997:* On Saturdays sat in individual meetings with his women graduate students—there were only two, whom I remember; and another one we met in Cambodia. He was aware of the gauntlet they ran and spoke of

it—and this *created* a gauntlet for me. But it was good that he spoke.]—
but my mother *gave* the dinner parties where the men sat at the table
and made the remarks.

She was flamboyant and beautiful.

I vowed speaking to myself, "I will always answer," meaning answer
baiting or humiliating mockery. I think I was on the playground when I
thought this. [*Nov. 2, 1997:* Later, I had the impression that I was re-
quired, a form of communing, to deal with this in the 'public world'—
required by my father and myself.]

[*Oct. 28, 1997:* Laughing, my mother told later that at the age of five
I said "I'm going to have two husbands, one to raise the children and
one to pay attention to *me*."]

At school at age six, I stood on the playground watching the girls
chase a cluster of boys, including Jimmy Cooper whom I loved, into a
distant corner of the playground to encircle and kiss them. I grasped
what socially is, what would be expected of me, and rejected it.

There was no anger felt or comprehended by me in this rejection.

Standing on the playground as they chased to encircle I said interi-
orly, "I will always be myself."

[*Oct. 29, 1997:* Prepared to give up others' way of behavior (as giving
up being in communion with them). Yet Jimmy Cooper kissed me as we
walked home from school, so this indicates one will be free, not 'be' be-
havior (despite the movie *Red Shoes* which I was taken to see about four
or so times because of the dancing—as also taken to see *The Wizard of
Oz*, about seven times, carried screaming from it at age four, then took
to it—but *Red Shoes* the woman who is the ballerina, being required to
give up her career or he will leave her, he leaves she runs to the balcony
overlooking the train station where he is far off walking; stretching to
see him, she falls under the wheels of the train).

There was a tremendous conflict implied—as if interior, being 'free'
paired to this conflict at the same time (i.e. being 'free' is simultaneous
with the conflict).

At that age: 'I'd risk the train rather than 'not to do what one needs
to'.']

[*Oct. 31, 1997:* This (that is, risking) is like my mother.]

After school I ran home and told my mother, "I decided today that I
will be myself" (words to that effect). She looked at me enthusiastically,
expectant as if to receive an explanation; when none came, said "Good!"
She had [has] a characteristic of not needing the answer.

Brave. Strong, asking for protection, slightly later asking for advice when I was too young to give it and not following it anyway. Competing with my father. The opposite of him in nature—her viewing her nature as superior and his as in need of change (his being quiet, as if a structure, of concentration—hers tending not to have type of attention but having spirit and will). They have a lifetime bond of love. She would criticize him intensely, his nature, to me and tell me I was the same as him; she would be protected (by him).

[*Oct. 28, 1997:* After traveling these are separate strands yet then entwined, 'one' being the same person as him exactly when he's alive, a reincarnation in his present.]

After traveling, that is overlaid with hordes of beggars vulnerable to dying—protecting people from dying, not oneself, also viewed as if interiorly. Without speaking it because the spatial nature of it can't be expressed that way. Sense of necessity to protect *her*—from these men who baited.

Later expressed in writing as if a spatial relation—serious and laughing as in the same tone, *Mother India*. [*Nov. 8, 1997:* There's a leap—between—to Cindy Sherman's photos now.]

We went to all these operas too, people taking a long time to die, moving us as music, not the plot-line. [*Oct. 29, 1997:* Intense expression, *being* the music, the sound, rather than the story.] My mother sang in concerts, practicing at home. My older sister and I played the piano, sang in choir; my younger sister sang. My mother took me to the opera. When I was in high school I went to the opera by myself, standing in the back.

The writing as comprehending at the same moment (as itself) that this (expressions of extremity) was something to unlearn. One as if getting ready to unlearn it.

My father played opera continually while thundering on his typewriter til 2:00 or 3:00 a.m. When I was six I was aware of him rushing down the stairs at some such hour past my bedroom (stopping to listen to the sound of my coughing, then continuing when I stopped) on his way to get coffee which he'd take up to his study; the blast shaking music gave one the sense of security in sleep when sometimes waking.

[*Nov. 8, 1997:* Tom Raworth was staying at our house—Oct. 25—and we went to see Masami Teraoka's new paintings, AIDS series, as if a weightless surface that is also akin to Bosch.]

Early memory (five or six?) of driving in a large car through Los Angeles seated in the back seat with my mother's mother, her husband driving, my mother beside him in front, and my taking my grandmother's hand to hold it.

My grandmother removed my hand from hers, and placing her fingers on my arm dug into my arm pinching it with her fingers and nails as hard as she could; while causing me excruciating pain she gazed into my face gleefully.

I said nothing during this. Then she gave my arm back to me with a significant look as if "so there" or "take that."

I had no spoken-thoughts gazing into her face, which was gleeful because causing me pain and watching me see its intentionality. Yet my saying nothing, not crying—was a response that was a thought. I had the sense this wasn't human and that if I thought it wasn't human, it meant I had the sense of 'something that is human.' Like waking up crying tying one's shoe. [*Nov. 14, 1997:* 'Someone has given me an idea of "human,"' but also implies *anything* could be human.]

I wasn't frightened or angry. Certainly wary. I didn't ever dislike her.

My parents not only had large dinner parties, but we lived with Japanese, Korean, or Kenyan students, sometimes several at a time; and for several years with students and my father's brother, Uncle Bill.

A Japanese student living with us when I was in elementary school (I had the sense of him being at my age, being along with me, though he was an adult), had been a Kamikaze pilot at age fifteen, called up for his mission. World War II ended three days before he was to fly; he was so amped for it he was shattered then, in response to not going (dying).

He painted pictures of Mt. Fuji for me, sitting in my small chair, children's chair. He had an egoless nature as his actions and the impression he made. At the time, I had the sense—not simply: willing to die, but risking (engaging in open recognition of) what occurs in fact anyway—is what 'men' are; oneself not being different from that characteristic.

My grandmother, Mimi, holding both of our hands when surrounded by beggars who are wailing as they push against the cart.

Her reading to us in Japan.

Crashing their sides together laughing, my father and Mimi, walking up a hotel hall toward us, who'd put our heads out of the door to greet them, in Taiwan when I was seven.

Summers, we took the Greyhound Bus to stay with Mimi in Santa Barbara, being taken to the beach. Her giving the impression that communion with people is known before, is a given. As if one *knew* what it *is* before (knew *that* it is).

My father, and on other occasions his brother, Uncle Bill, consented to play "the picking game" in which my sisters and I encircled and with our fingers picked on the person, finally dragging them down while they screamed and laughed.

Uncle Bill, warm tyrannical-Italian-family-style-demeanor-of-man (intellectual macho, as well as macho) had a witty teasing humor; very passionate, volatile anger sometimes unfair, many tempestuous romances (as well as three marriages and four children). He couldn't be dragged to the ground; arrived roaring to put us on the bus to Santa Barbara when our cousins were mistreating us (our parents in Asia); threw away our Classic Comic Book collection, so carefully acquired, because it was rotting our minds.

My father, very passionate, volatile anger, liking to argue politically as mode of contact—did allow us to drag him down, laughing and shrieking. We went to see *Harvey, the Six-foot Rabbit* and I was watching my father laugh as much as watching the movie.

My first boyfriend, at Reed College, resembled this combination.

Uncle Bill once standing, arguing politically with my father, kept swaying his hips to distract him and win.

My mother, while not needing 'to know the answer'—ever—only the act itself occurring, at the same time had intricate rules (for cleaning house, for the 'right way to do things,' or right order) which while one starting as a tiny child scrutinized her, the source of the trajectories of rules, these were undecipherable, seemed to have no application or basis.

Only the rules 'having no basis' in fact—'at all'—jived with beggars running alongside the train car, with men running pulling rickshas or men lifting very heavy loads manually destitute otherwise, i.e., frighteningly close to dying *per se*.

She would, for example, have me vacuum the same room over again automatically (so that I knew I would have to do it again, no matter how well I did it), to vacuum dust that wasn't there—I learned from this 'there are no rules'—no rules govern anything, at all. This was the only relief. My response at the same time as my freaking out was, "whoopi" (in regard to having no rules).

Attempting to distract one to prevent one from concentrating—on what one needs to have attention to.

My second boyfriend (at Reed College), while a passionate relation, passionate tie, did continual contradictory, emotionally chaotic moves and orchestrating of events—trying to de-rail one from concentration, to control it, so one could not be oneself. I didn't see this while it was occurring or even after breaking up with him, the actions being chaotic as 'unseen.' Predisposition that 'he's' *actually* oneself, recurrences in the same time, neither is before the other. 'So' waking once after dreaming of him, I wanted to murder him. Not because I then would not be controlled, but because I would not be in chaos—if he were not at all. i.e., I was not controlled, I was in chaos.

Earlier, 'shapes' were in actions in the exterior world.

Playing leap-frog—being deliberately kicked by the team going over one—until one had to react.

Then surrounded, hair-pulling, chest being pushed, their screaming—someone: "she called you a nigger" knowing one'd been silent, one shouting back surrounded "you're lying you're lying." (I thought that I 'was them,' 'exactly them'—'recognized' one kid feeling strongly that I 'had known him before,' though I could not have, because I hadn't known anyone who was African American before and had had only a short life. I wanted to be one with them. Although I could not in any way be accepted, some girls noticed puzzled, thinking it was unusual but okay?)

In writing, one would have to interiorize this action to have it be action in one reading.

One being accepted because one had shouted back—'if one is not social, one is not in existence' (I thought the Greeks thought).

(For each game there'd be appointed a white and a black volleyball or speedball team captain who would call the names of teammates to bring them to her side; but the Black kids would only play on the Black captain's team, going over to that side no matter where they were called. Perhaps the teacher should have designated two Black captains.)

Driving in the Philippines at night in the war burial ground millions of graves shining—being on a ship from one Philippine island to another.

Sleeping on deck in the heat, on the lower deck a herd of pigs slipped and swayed, their scent coming to the cots if the wind changed. A pig died on the deck, we had pork. Docking at one island, then moving on.

Traveling (age thirteen), we were crossing from India to East Africa on a ship on which were many Indian and African college students returning to their countries from Indian universities.

The ship was segregated, whites were in first class; though we were in second class with Indian families, the women sequestered unseen, never allowed from the hot cabins while their men strolled on deck leaning on the railing seeing the ocean.

Two Indian women were diagnosed with smallpox; their husbands had not allowed them to go to a doctor to be vaccinated. We weren't allowed to disembark at some ports because we were quarantined, though passengers and stevedores boarded.

In the heat passengers decided to swim off the side of the ship; but changed their minds seeing the white fins of sharks circling the ship.

The college students were all in third class until we began to be friends, conversing on the second class deck where we played cards.

One night a dance was given on the second class deck, my older sister, mother, and myself the only 'women' who danced. No whites (besides us) would dance because non-whites were participating on the second class deck; the whites sat looking down from the top deck in stony silence.

Encircled by the seated crowd, my older sister and I with our partners the only couples dancing then, two young African men (the students themselves used the word "African" not wanting to emphasize the nation or tribe from which they came); my partner shook so violently his legs could barely move, sweat pouring down him, while I was calm, younger, outsider.

My older sister and I next day were stopped and smashed against the wall near the ship's store by South African fat whites glaring out of little inflamed eyes hatefully.

My father was asked by the students to lecture and did so in the dining hall, where no one ate except us because of their various customs; (the first time of my listening to a lecture by him) he talked about nationalism and colonialism, colonized nations freeing themselves from imperialism.

I recall him delineating the example of Britain having sent students from its colonies to universities in Britain, where the students learned revolution against Britain. I thought he meant me. I thought it was a direct instruction to rebel by being taught.

At each port where we stopped along the coast of East Africa, the students who lived in the particular country would disembark. We waved goodbye leaning on the ship's railing to one, whom we'd nicknamed "John-I.M.G." (for "John-Imperialism-Must-Go") who as he walked away raised his fist saying goodbye and in front of the white South Africans hanging on the railing looking down, said "Imperialism must go." He spent years in a British prison; I watched while my mother packed books to send him and others, one of these Thoreau's *Civil Disobedience*.

Because of these actions and my father being on the blacklist, we were not allowed to enter South Africa, were put off the ship in Mozambique. Having purchased a car waiting in Johannesburg, we'd been going to drive across Africa, through the Sudan to Egypt; so we drove *in* Africa, took planes to Khartoum and Cairo.

On a boat crossing a river in Rhodesia, a fat white man seated alone by my older sister and I and by a kneeling man steering, provoked by our being from 'outside,' vilely abused being Black as inferior, and brutal bullying action to the three of us, the "African" boatman turning his face away from the man so that his face was visible to us, tentative clear expressionless.

It was being between. Spatially. Gyration where one is there breathless, in violence. Later-beginning of one being in rage, the tendency to be adamant. Goaded. Associated with the men at the dinner table bullying. In Mozambique, I saw each evening a Portuguese man at the dinner table bullying his one-year-old son and wife, the latter responding with fear protecting the son.

[*Oct. 30, 1997*: In East Africa, green bright Congo with red earth, I was reading Huxley's *Evolution in Action*, which—there is no authority in one or outside, as *being* one's scrutiny—corroborated reading about Buddhism shortly before.

'That nothing is known'—being in the instant—is my sense of Zen, not 'belief'—the opposite.

This provoked later and right then rejection of customs, of having any at all—kneeling on the stained street in an overflow crowd of kneeling people at a cathedral, Easter mass in Bombay (we weren't Catholic either, we weren't anything)—some interior-jag of rejection occurred.

Must of been partly because we were asked to participate with, to have, 'other' customs that were not interior—were not 'one'—not 'action' really (as intrinsic).

Before being in India, standing in a plaza singing "God Save the Queen" when the governor of Hong Kong appeared in his coat-tails, I became simply furious.

I went to San Francisco by myself on the bus one day and saw a drunken unconscious man lying on the sidewalk be spat upon by a boy riding a bicycle by him back and forth to spit on him. Extremely disturbed, I told about this to my mother who jeered "You're like Gotama Buddha going out into the world for the first time" (i.e., 'stand the existence'—as far as I know, my mother didn't know I thought about Buddhism; I didn't speak of it—she was sarcastic). I was stung, and had the sense of not meeting reality.]

My parents founded a group called "The Committee for African Students," which brought students to attend school in Berkeley and placed them in homes of families. Several of the committee members were conductors on Amtrak railway. One member was Eugene Jones, a bass singer, later director of the Berkeley Community Orchestra, and earlier the first Black fireman in Berkeley. My mother had concerts at the house; Eugene Jones shook the house with that incredible melodious bass.

There were constant meetings—my mother thrived—there was only social in existence.

I was freaking out because how could there be being enlightened—as necessity—and there being no authority in one.

Hope Cook with (her husband soon after) the Prince of Sikkim (a country in the Himalayas, it is now part of India), on a Buddhist holiday so she stirred her plate of chicken with her fork without eating, came to lunch, and seated across from her I watched transfixed while she being disbelieved and condescended to throughout the conversation by a professor seated next to her at the table, keenly aware I was watching her (i.e., doing this for me, including me, bringing me in) indicated without animosity or response *that she just didn't give a shit, overtly that she just didn't give a shit.*

As if to say, this is possible. This is how you do it. (Dealing with him.) I was tremendously impressed.

At that time, I went to see Greek tragedies in Greek at U.C. Berkeley's Greek Theater. Read constantly, saw plays like *Waiting for*

*Godot;* Godard films, Igmar Bergman, Kurasawa, many others. Read Homer, Aeschylus, Sophocles, Euripides, Ibsen, Tolstoy, Dostoyevsky, Henry James, William James, many books about concentration camps (*Human Behavior in the Concentration Camp*) and World War II. I read all of Mao's sayings, pamphlets which I found in my father's study; and for a class at Berkeley High wrote a paper comparing Plato's view of art in the Republic to Mao's view of the place of art in the Republic.

The teacher, thrilled, read the entire essay to the class, punctuating his reading with exclamations that this one boy in the class was going to be a poet and I was going to be a scholar. I thought "I want to be a poet."

My friend leaving the class screamed at me that I was a vegetable, walking down the hall screaming over and over "You may know about Mao and Plato but you are nothing, you are a ve-ge-ta-ble" screamed. I never spoke to her again, except once briefly years later, encountering her crossing Sproul Plaza (UC), when she (taking a course from my father) oozed "he's so brilliant."

Driving, my father, at the time of my Mao paper, was stopped by the Berkeley police solely because he was a white man driving in a car with men who were Black.

[*Oct. 30, 1997:* My mother passed a rule that we had to attend church each Sunday until we were eighteen, which resulted in tempestuous battles and philosophical dispute each Sunday.]

My father used to chase us through the house shouting—we ran sometimes out the back door or into the bathroom which could be locked. This was unnerving [*Nov. 12, 1997:* indicating provocation as a mode, 'directing' "fight"]. But it was not frightening to me, my having the view that I was him, the same thing (also 'myself nothing').

My older sister, overtly rebellious, cut school, riding on the back of a motorcycle with her boyfriend. She went to the San Francisco Art Institute, eloping and marrying.

She had (has) a directness of behavior that short-circuits a situation— in the heat driving in Manila (no adults except the friend's chauffeur), the Philippine friend our age brings ice cream cones back to the car without bringing one for the chauffeur. At the houses there, waited on surrounded by ten servants—a servant would run all the way across the house to answer the phone placed by our friend, which was for her—we couldn't tolerate people waiting on us—here, Diane hands the ice cream cone to the chauffeur, "Here. Eat this."

I went to Reed College (Portland, Oregon). Which I loved (I think

they were teaching us how not what to think—to scrutinize construc-
tions creating history, not to accept these as information)—staying up
all night studying and writing papers—it was the first time of having
friends, the mist on the lawn in the morning when one was walking
across it; films in the chapel used as the theater/lecture hall: *The Seven
Samurai, Ivan the Terrible*, Warhol's *Sleep*.

[*Nov, 11, 1997: As being held in conflict—as control of one*—One who
hasn't done this is Charles Bernstein.

In one of my earliest conversations with him—without him being
aware of anyone there but the person to whom he was speaking—he said
as his observation "You are the person/the protagonist in *Loneliness of the
Long-distance Runner*."

I was taken aback because I'd seen this film and identified with the per-
son—who, from a lower class British context, was chosen by his teacher to
race against the upper class twits who jeered at him and at those from his
social class; yet he chooses to lose (and be held in his lower class condi-
tion) being much faster than they are (running, he was going to win).

I said nothing in the conversation with Charles because I was sur-
prised, yet either losing or joining is impossible. I think he may have
meant '*refuses* to join related to that specific conflict, being that specific
conflict.'

'and oneself being controlled by being in conflict'—(my description).

[Earlier, my father was attacked by Un-American Activities McCar-
thy for his view on China. Was an Adlai Stevenson democrat. Once, he
was credited by the Koreans for helping to spark a revolution in South
Korea by outlining how this might occur in a speech before the Senate
Foreign Relations Committee. Copies of the speech banned in Korea,
an 'American school teacher' in Korea asked for a letter, which he
sent. Actually, the one who requested the copy, after instigating the
revolution, was the next president of Korea.]

In the Vietnam War—my father (as an advisor on Asia to Presidents
Kennedy, Johnson; later Carter, Reagan, and Clinton) favored US mili-
tary intervention—I disagreed with this; and also interpret his view as
determined by his fear of what was going to later occur in Vietnam and
in Cambodia, genocide—

Ever since—now even, frequently—men defining me to myself
'through' his 'views'—though they may not know what these are.

i.e. One is in reference only to a man. In their view. And answerable
to 'their' prior definition based on view of someone else—not there.

Figure 6. Author at 25 or so.

If they could not use this, these men (also, sometimes women) would attempt to control by using something else. Phantom. Which they *do* with others.

If I respond I am 'reacting' merely—am not 'one'—either, whether reacting to them (or if I were reacting to him).

Yet it is not him trying to hold me to his views. This is not related to that war.]

OCT. 30, 1997

*Considering how exaggerated music is* is a collection (1975–1982) of works that were very hard to write—because they were under heavy emotional pressure, and were very understated as the means of withstanding that, and conveying it. Yet conveying the emotion is not what they were (are); it was as if a reed instrument blowing dual notes at once—in which if the instrument *is* emotion, one wonders (I was wondering) what emotion is itself.

The pieces of this book were like music—dissonant notes being played at the same spot throughout; or a slightly 'contrary' note follows an initiating note (sometimes divided by the word "although")—the notes 'then' (there, in the spot) are not connected yet imply something common to neither.

Where events or emotional strands are drastic they are either high or low musical notation or both at once.

Lines are cool tonally and conceal events being extremely 'funny' as a faculty of 'event itself.' Rather, having motion in events that is a faculty.

So emotion (such as 'funny') is not a known. Only by 'those modes' is there a "public world," i.e. where there is no separation.

*This eating and walking at the same time is associated all right* (a poem in that collection) was influenced by listening to Coltrane for the first time, and listening over and over—and also (at once) traveling for the first time in the U.S., on Greyhound buses in the Midwest and Nevada. A sentence in it (in poems throughout) linked by the word "though" is both phrases qualifying the other though logically this isn't occurring— 'to recur' and 'that there isn't relation ever' is 'qualifying.'

> Unemployed though when I heard someone who used an obscene word the
> other day
> he didn't look as if he were in another world
> and so I'm worried
> especially in this sultry weather.

I wrote without plan and without any sense that I knew what this was or was going to be. I always write that way, and here I had the sense that the writing was separate from and alongside anything (events that were extreme), the writing was a light extremity. It was the first time I was writing.

Events were light extremities—serious so that they were simply gone—I wasn't there any more (at the time).

One walked through Berkeley—Vietnam vets were distracted done-in on the street—a truck being unloaded of Vietnamese in wheelchairs, which I walked through, paraplegics, quadriplegics, their heads bobbing like petals, expressions of being grateful and meek—blowing one away. I had left being married—knew no one for the time, all friends left—

stayed in my crow's nest on Etna St. sometimes for days (doing odd jobs for a living), because no money sometimes no food, or only a little—only an orange once. It was a relief. A light vacancy in which or because I was in overt pain. It was *not* muffled because of a man I knew 'not for long' (met after leaving being married), which enabled an extremity to occur in a light vacancy outside, made it be that. Dogs began to do odd things when I walked by—following me all across Berkeley—beginning to dance in disturbance at me—or run rising to nip my jacket—the dream of the dog tracking me recurred.

This was at the time of writing *hmmmm* (in *Considering how exagger-ated music is*).

My mother was in a car accident just after this, a wreck in which Mimi was killed and mother was paralyzed from the waist down.

I 'saw' a coffin, the result of an 'accident,' in a room, which I was see-ing writing in a poem when the accident was occurring. When I got to Mimi's funeral, coming from the hospital in Salinas where I'd seen my mother, Mimi's coffin (purchased by my younger sister) was the same I'd seen in the same room.

I had a dream three days later in which Mimi as a flesh-silhouette was traveling slowly up a hill with her face turned to the side, her face seen from the side. Not communicating with me.

She knew she was going to die. When Uncle Bill came to my parent's front door to say goodbye to her, she'd opened the door and said "Oh, I thought you were the archangel coming to get me." I was just leaving and she stuffed a portable radio into my hands and said "Here, you have this" (i.e. this is from me).

[*Nov. 6, 1997*: This dream of Mimi with the face turned to the side with sense of location and my knowing that she's dead has recurred ever since—the last time two years ago: traveling in China on a boat on the Yangtze River studying Dōgen's view of 'time as being' or 'being as time,' I had a dream in which I was trying to travel between locations to get a friend, whom I hadn't seen or heard from for ten years, to have lunch with Mimi whose face was now not turned to the side and whom I didn't realize was dead; the man's face was turned to the side, and then he wouldn't go to lunch—waking, I thought he had died.

The man called me after I returned and said "I had a dream about you, in which we were going to go to lunch but then we didn't." I real-ized that in terms of 'being as time' 'all times, past, future, present, being at the same time' the dream was my process of studying this—it wasn't that the man was dead; it was that she isn't in death except when she died, spatially she isn't in death now. [Yet still she's not alive!]

This was part of the spatial sense that was coming about in a poem I was writing then (on the Yangtze River) called *Friendship* that is for Lyn Hejinian. Lyn indicating something to me about relation between people; occurring spatially—the relation *is* the time—her rendering that.

[*Nov. 11, 1997:* I got the sense from her of a relation to people, of being with others, as 'friendship'—changing space it's in, being that space, outside of people even.

The space is changed or expanded so that the conflict of one being nonexistent if one is not 'social'/public isn't occurring. Change as space only, there.]

In *The Front Matter, Dead Souls*, I was trying to write real political-social events transpiring at the time, written only as visual text (with no pictures). The images are to be bulbous, 'extreme' vivid in the sense of their being 'of' eyesight only, as if existing apart from any 'event' that is written-meaning. As if *by* being that which is physical seeing only, rather than their being language-imagination (i.e. as if they *could* be only physical seeing only as text, and are not imagination), the events are seen 'without imposition as my imagination' (i.e. it is actually total imposition—one is seeing constructing, and seeing 'not seeing constructing' by 'seeing' being 'visual' which is actually only-language).

This can only be done as poetic writing.

Events occur before the words; one has to translate from a medium that is without any words. The sense that one can grasp that which is transmitting from others—is less authority-based than the 'authority of the prior word'? (Less authority-based than any description; or than borrowing another text as basis of the writing. Though a borrowed text could noticeably leak *its* memory onto the new text, thus showing constructing of memory.) Present 'events' are more 'subjective' and less fixed because they exist in the present instant?

If one places everything on this level—'subjective'—and sees what happens.

Akin to Bob Grenier's hand-drawn poems that are the motion or gesture of their line-as-drawing (more drawing than handwriting—the lines some times on each other in different colors) which are text as only silent.

'Life'/as occurrence as silent—or 'not itself' *per se.*

The writing is doing the (exact) same motions 'conceptually'—*so that* one is not in one's life:

So that one is not in one's life. So it has an impossible relation to it.

Describing now various events of one's life—these are not to be demonstrated, elucidated, described, or the subject of the writing later, or before, or then.

Dreaming is a separate action—a spatial occurrence. Waking up tying one's shoe.

Later—writing *that they were at the beach* and *way* I was frantically trying to get the motions (as words separated by dashes and in line breaks) to be minutely the same—which is separate per se.

In the writing the writing was the same actions—only. At some point I was desperate; now I do not reenter that state of mind—which is intrinsic conflict as itself an action of the writing in the real 'outside'—that is tied to—detached from freely—itself—that is a joy—or being serene—walking by / oneself, as: alongside, freely.]

[*Oct. 31, 1997:* Trying to sleep—before going to see my mother in Intensive Care—was the frame rising off the bed horizontal sleeping—early morning. Separate from the sense of the thin flattened car wreck frame in space.

My father would always be out ahead, with cameras (slung on him, or jetting ahead with camera in hand)—in Mongolia, say. Analyzing something in terms of what it is, not how it is described.

His same intense gesture inside, and outside itself lightly—as being what the outside is. Our differences having to do with basis that is authority—or there not *being* a basis of authority (differing in our sense of that). He and I'd eat in Chinese restaurants in Salinas by the hospital. Hands me Mimi's blood-soaked sweater to wash in the tub.

My parents continue to travel constantly returning to China, to Hanoi, to Mongolia. My father's a 'negotiator' with North Korea in relation to South Korea and to famine and conditions in the North.

Having a thin public existence—in precarious livelihood—yard work, sweeping in dirt—walking in the light vacancy—in fall—others there—young also and won't speak—not the parasites on them. The one's who have social parasites attached to them and young. This all occurring in one time as writing, that is numerous social episodes. One'd see some go by, who won't speak. It is not describing—but analyzing from the inside—is based on the thin public existence itself. Their being one.

NOV. 1, 1997

"Unless we are not experience" (*Orion*).

One is not one's experience. I wanted (want) to not be one's experience—separated from it—something is occurring. Yet there is the disjunct moment outside—isn't one or it's not disjunct.

This morning I reread *Orion* (in *The Return of Painting, The Pearl, and Orion / A Trilogy*, because it just arrived reprinted by Talisman Publishers) in which there is this same episode earlier here, of waking up tying one's shoe.

I forget I'd written a reference and repeat it somewhere. Seeing what comes up 'now.' The characteristic of *Trilogy* is that single lines as paragraphs occur as if a long series—such as events from finite memory (of the individual)—but (implication of) infinite numbers of fictional events are there.

I'd just put in memories not as accounts but as finite series that gets to the point of infinite—as 'fictional' it can't be remembered / isn't memory, at all.

[*Nov. 8, 1997:* The cover of the *Trilogy* has one of my photos, a figure (Tom White) naked, with his back to the viewer and facing out into a desert landscape, which was near the DIA Walter de Maria Lightning Rod Field in New Mexico—as if the real landscape is the Hudson School of painting, a reverse order.]

About a year after my mother's accident, I met Tom White.

[*Nov. 2, 1997:* We've lived together since then, marrying eleven years after we met.

Considering motion:—in Baja on a cliff at night surrounded by horses brushing its strings—in a tent on a cliff—is spatially separated from and occurring as, a serenity in his nature (which I was trying to apprehend as a pair—in the writing; I'd try to get that 'pair in his nature' which is itself in 'action-outside,' i.e. action being itself that pair).

Action and his nature as the same:

                    —to
notice
          'reverse grace'—him—love

early fan
outer walking
early

Also political-social apprehended in his nature, being it, as a serene
aspect in (of) seeing it; i.e. is in his apprehension in which the element of
chaos or violence in event is not negated or overlooked.

          breaks past rungs while in their middle—
dawn's
          his—people's—fleeing camps—one's
bursting—'in' it—separate—is—on his

          his quiet's
[[his] 'heart's'—valve] burst 'on'—a—dawn time—one's

There's a sense that the thin real landscape 'as' the instant 'of' one
'as' him can be the same 'as' early. That which is outside has no base as
one—that is: as one doesn't either.

          his base walks
          one's—there's a space—in
between like throwing
          —dawn's-trees-fan—is—early-instant's

space—this instant in
          the same
one—one's base walks—
          his-thin
moon's-day early          (From: *Zither*)

Aspects of him as being actions—one moves off even being actions, is
not even actions—so traveling is not the basis—driving in the spring
countryside in India between Jaipur and Agra; he and I were riding in a
bus through Calcutta with multitudes working, hammering, bathing
(*Defoe*, chapter "Black Orchid"); driving in Yemen by white soft sand
dunes or in rainless desert where plastic bags stopped and clung; in
Egypt and the Sudan; on trains in Japan, him resting or waiting in snow

by a Zen temple in Kyoto; in a jeep in Bhutan by blossoming Himalayan rhododendron trees.

[*Nov. 8, 1997:* Driving in Italy forward in the balls of pollen flying towards us.

Together watching Noh in Japan. I think, as a young woman, I equated one trying for being 'enlightened' and ever having the mystery of being in love as related.

In Bhutan inside the main temple with Tom and my parents, I saw the yearly Buddhist dances performed by monks in animal and deity masks and costumes.

Yet during one day of the dances outside I went by myself and in order to see scrambled up on a cliff side, my clinging on a small dirt ledge, above me a plateau of hundreds of seated small children.

Slightly larger children standing on my feet came to cling to the same ledge; as if flying out from the cliff side when the figure of death entered the dance.

We stood on the ledge watching for four hours, the Bardo dance, the crowd itself entering to bow amongst the dancers when death entered.

We could see the structure and entering and leaving above them as if right on them flying.

As the public bowing was there in that moment, Westerners came up putting their cameras in the faces to take pictures. In the midst of the dance, the Westerners refused to withdraw. [They were mocking them, as if their beliefs were primitive.]

In *As: All Occurrence in Structure, Unseen—(Deer Night)* which I wrote after this, I wanted to have some interior sense of this other (Bhutan) culture, which is 'oneself interiorly—coming apart,' transform the outer culture which is here (one's own culture).

I'd just include whatever was happening as it was occurring alongside anything else occurring (written: as visual-memory which are sound-shapes) without movements or events having any conclusion or shape that I knew.

In the structure, the 'minute' would not be a basis—though it was the only ground.

A man seated alone his horse bowed by him on an illumined vast gold land—it changing, illumined from the sky alone—which is indigo.

This was while crossing Mongolia (with my parents and Tom) in two jeeps.

NOV. 7, 1997

Gail Sher and I used to go together to visit Philip Whalen* (I still do), once having a 'session to discuss' *The Tale of Genji* and Japanese Heian civilization.

I love Japanese poetic diaries and monogatari particularly of the Heian period (Middle Ages), these indicating a view of the self which while being sometimes intense clinging is visible as not entity in the continuing structure.

So it's wondering what one is.

In *way*, I was influenced by the structure of poetic diaries as poem/prose pairs—I wanted, in the structure throughout and in the minute unit (only one or two words on a line) as order of perception (past and present reverberating back into the 'past' of the poem's structure at any one point at the same time as into its future—disrupting—serene at once) occurring in the line breaks, *to have* impermanence, to seek this—actively—as a gesture in the world, outside of oneself, not 'about' events being one.

And that minute 'duplication' as events simply go out and out, not re-curring as a prior known shape.

[Some interior configuration was occurring, the urgency of which was 'one is not oneself for even an instant'—should not be. One *must* not be 'one,' change throughout. Disrupt the continuance of any characteristic or mode in 'one.' Then, disrupting interior was interfering with writing, living.

Serial thinking—that nothing recurs or is in/crosses the same place—yet is going on.

Sight, color, emotion, as if in the *act of its present-time* placed on the level of 'logic,' are also forms of logic qualifying occurrence.

My writing 'the act of an emotion or sight in its present-time/as it qualifies its own occurrence even'—was said by others to be "merely" narrative of emotional experience. I would try to say this. This drove me 'outside it' to attempt it again. ]

---

*Knowing people, with no authority between them. One of the most important people in my life, Philip passed away on June 26, 2002.

Figure 7. 1985. *Photo by Tom White.*

[Again. Syntax is *entirely* different from physical motion. Thus (in early works, through the 1980s) I wanted the writing to be that gap: the writing *being* life, real-time minute motions (physical movements or events) but being or *are* these (minute motions) *as syntax* (abstraction, not representation).

Syntax is memory trace or conceptual shape. Yet it was to replace, or to be, the (its) present-time motion only. It can't be a memory, or a life then.

By implication, to apprehend the present time, the world, changing, means tracking it in its (every) instant. Not leadership of intellectuals or artists only. Anyone see the present entire world changing. Many are seeing at once.

In my later works, *New Time* (written 1995–1998) and *The Tango* (written 1999–2000), I wanted to heighten (which erases?) the gap separating oneself and action, so that (as the writing) many events might be occurring at once, with no separation between oneself and dawn (or word) or night, one not separate from phenomena. Writing is phenomena.

My description of *The Tango*, a poem which I placed in vertical strips alongside photos I took of monks at the Sera Monastery in Tibet engaging in formal debate: "The text's internal debate is the author's 'comparison' of *her* mind phenomena to exterior phenomena, laying these alongside each other 'actually'—such as the mind's comparison to dawn, to magnolias, to color of night, as if these are manifestations of mind phenomena, which they are *here*. Placing one's mind-actions beside magnolias (words). The same figure repeated everywhere, a line or passage may recur exactly as slipping out of, returning, slipping out of, a frame of concentration and sound."]

Rick London and I were in a reading group, which first started at the Hartford Zen Center, studying especially Huang Po and Nāgārjuna; it lasted three or four years, by the end all the original members of the group (except myself and London) dying of AIDS. These people and the opportunity to concentrate on the reading matter were crucial to me.

[*Nov. 11, 1997:* Remembering one man plunging in the wheelchair— in the zendo—unable to control any of his limbs.

Issan (Thomas Dorsey), who himself died of AIDS, during the time of the reading group created an AIDS hospice at Hartford in San Francisco.

Earlier, Issan taught me the gestures of sitting, me resistant to the concept of bowing, wanting to know the concept—"What are we bowing to?"—"What are you bowing to? Whatever you want."

Issan describing once being stopped by the Chicago police for driving at 80 mph under the influence through Chicago, asked to walk a line—emerged from the car in full drag wearing highheels; made some humorous remark to the police, which I don't remember, as to why he couldn't walk or talk ("I have a speech impediment").

He wasn't describing a ritual, in bowing or sitting, but rather one's gesture *then*. After saying (it's addressed to, it means) "Whatever you want," he added helpfully "*You* should bow" (meaning 'whose authority are you responding to?' 'don't have authority.' 'Do what you are unable to do.')

Huang Po: "those who seek the goal through cognition are like the

Figure 8. Tom White, author's husband.

fur (*many*), while those who obtain intuitive knowledge of the Way are like the horns (*few*)."

'having *cognition* in the writing occur as intuitive faculty *only*' (and intuition occur as cognitive faculty only).]

[*Nov. 12, 1997:* This intersected, in the poem-play *leg*, with Trojan women falling from burning slides.]

Rick writing would also read what others were writing in the moment and do so in a rigorous manner as a sociable quality. As would Ted Pearson. Readings would go on, everyone giving readings and talks.

[*Nov. 14, 1997:* One stuck out her long pink tongue at me while one of her friends reading was satirizing various poets; the satire on me was 'on' Artaud (because I was teaching a class on him) as if we were the same and that was extreme (his sensibility or viewpoint, negativity and insanity)—the satirist (who'd concluded jeering, "*I'm* not sensitive.") later taught Artaud, probably not remembering the aforementioned.]

Ron Silliman a very vital poet; later, I also enjoyed arguing with him trying to change his mind in our exchange about 'one' in writing in relation to 'social being' (women being caught in oppression having less incentive, in his opinion, for radical apprehension, form as writing. That people's emotion is convention per se? Thus viewed by him as "conventional narrative"), published in the *Poetics Journal*. "You refuse to question self," Ron wrote in a letter to me earlier (before the *Poetics Journal* exchange, around the time of women jumping falling from burning walls). My view being that of anyone *having to* (have such apprehension, non-normative language), it is demanded. Because one has to articulate outside the language of social conscription in order to be outside any (one has to occur before) definition—occurring as exchange there. Or exchange, the social world, does not occur at all? ['Early-walking as the same as T—T's early-walking is the space *there*' real-time. Alongside one waking at night terrified as one's not living *then* separate from it—'the instant' as 'not being with' him at all. Is 'the instant' real-time as not living at all? 'Submitting' events to serial thinking is qualifying the occurrences as the act of its present-time literally changing it. To do this-writing again and again.

Serial-thinking: to add single words to 'each other' so that the components retain their single meaning but 'by addition only' have at once an additional meaning. I.e. the text isn't (can't be) real-time. One's relation to "early" and one's relation to "walking" are retained (only as motion)—but only as 'him' in space—him existing.

'Single.' No possessive. Not to turn by intensity 'him' into one so there is only one. One being 'it not to be itself' *there*.]

Barrett Watten (I liked his poetry very much), with editor Lyn Hejinian, published my writing in *Poetics Journal*; as curator at New Langton Arts in San Francisco, he invited me to have a play produced there, *The Present*, directed by Zack (who also directed my play *The Weatherman Turns Himself In* and part of *Deer Night*).

—At a retrospective of Jasper Johns's painting, I thought the paintings were 'pure thought,' only—for an instant—(as: seen by someone—at some instant)—; not the contents being thought *about*. It seems to me this is what Barry's writing was doing when scrutinizing events-(as historical) in or as 'thought.'

Having respect, not to have models (but loving him). Once when

Philip Whalen walked me out to my car after visiting—I was wearing a casual jacket with my hands in the pockets—he remarked, speaking simply as a question (words to the effect) "Are you just going to be James Dean?"—'are you just going to continue to do that?'

I was struck by this—of course taken-aback—and so I put the image of James Dean as a character in *Defoe* who is in the midst of war, the converging of drug dealers on the Sudanese desert (i.e. has never happened), and transformed into a deer with antlers running in panic as bombs pock-mark the desert, so 'the other' who is the 'heroine' pursues through black rain to protect or rescue him, who is dead.

This was then enacted in the play *The Present* (which is passages from *Defoe*); Zack wore a James Dean mask and later appears with no mask wearing tree branches on a motorcycle helmet like antlers, his hands raised as if paws of the deer.

*Defoe*—Figures thrown as if walking on air on motorcycles thrown in air—one walking in a vast march in the streets of New York hemmed in by police on horseback—are narrowed 'horizontal rim' vertical spatial paragraphs the conceptual rim, observed sometimes in sitting. Sitting before freezing red leaves sea outside. The paragraph as a horizon rim on which one's actions (actual and also mind-actions at the same time) arise seen. Walking on boulevards and across bridges in Paris. Time of something actually occurring—is at all times of the text. Walking amidst columns of young beautiful North and West African prostitutes and tricks choosing them on a Paris side street.

In *Defoe*, there's no distinction *in time* as fiction, real events (it was in the midst of war, crowds), and optical seeing: "The bud's flattened on its own. Cattle come along side. They're standing in the sky on a small ledge but it's dusk. The disc is hanging behind them making them dark and flat from the front. The newspaper says a man in the sea was floated by a tortoise. This is the difference between event and what it says. The bud opens, seeing them, though it can't see."

The FDA for years stalled and blocked use of a method determining the AIDS virus load in patients, fouling this in red tape arising from their ignorance and aggressive habituation (saying they would never accept this until there is a cure), the method essential to use of the new AIDS drug treatments. Scientists Tom White and John Sninsky presenting over and over to the bureaucrats on the FDA panel, one time one bureaucrat fell asleep, another bureaucrat turning down acceptance of the method because he "could not understand it." The atmosphere then (while the one bureaucrat slept) charged, AIDS activists ACT-UP told there is no time for them to speak, rose anyway to speak. (After years, the diagnostic method was accepted for use in treatment.)

Carla Harryman's writings have been important to me. Reminds me of a dancer I saw, a wolverine whirling forward, the projectile there.

[*Nov. 14, 1997:* On Nov. 11—Not strong enough to drag my mother out of the car, with my back turned to her and her holding my waist, or to lower her into it on returning to the sidewalk—taking her to a doctor's appointment in Oakland, having to ask men who were passersby to lift her; could not take her out of the car returning home.]

On Nov. 13, I drove in El Niño, amidst sweeping tunnels and wafts of rain, car crashes everywhere, figures lying on the ground in the rain— at the sides of the highway, fire trucks and totaled cars—streaming cars pushing through this—from San Diego to L.A.

On the same day coming back vast clouds illuminated smoke-stacks pouring clouds also—on resting traffic lines.

In between, in L.A., I met my sister Diane and we went to the Bill Viola video installation retrospective at L.A. County Museum. There were sixteen rooms.

For example, "Reflecting Pool"—A screen hanging in the midst of a room, the same seen on either side, a man emerges from a forest and stands before a pool of water, the forest and man's figure reflected in it. He jumps up over the pool and at the instant his curled ball in air is still, and reflections of only the forest go on and change in the pool; or faint reflections of the man or other figures walking at the side of the pool and forest. Until the curled ball of man, that never enters the surface of pool, disappears.

There is no sound.

The images projected in the pool, separate from the curled projectile of the man which is never reflected 'have no source'—time also 'has no source' and is still, while the figures/perceptions, not those of the viewers either, are going on moving.

"Tiny Deaths"—Three large projections appear on the walls of a completely dark room—in which the indistinct dim human silhouettes emerge on a field of noise of voices murmuring; the silhouettes indistinguishable from this dim noise field as if a space that's 'glade' 'surfaced-forest' (as if they are the "shades" as in ancient Greek conception, the field of noise implying multitudes of such 'figures.').

Out of each of the dim figures—on its surface—becomes some articulated face and figure wearing a dress or wearing shirt and pants, illuminated white light as individual in slight motion which then bursts, momentarily illuminating the room and washing out the other two projections. Until the figures begin to emerge again in the darkness—and vanish as burst; as if in reverse surface they emerged out of 'shades' 'death' to then burst as 'instant.'

It's coming up to instant of 'one' in which even any state, 'death,' has been eliminated, being undergone, prior.

There's no future that's *either* death or life.

Coming back, vast clouds illuminated smoke-stacks pouring clouds also—on resting traffic lines.

The video installation can render real-time (i.e. that which we experience) as illusion.

Yet language can do that in some ways—'as if' murmured multiple voices—and silence of curled form without reflection, as if language could be silent—by being 'image of' 'ourselves' from outside.

Memory as visual that's only a 'present.' Silent because it's 'read' which is always 'past/present.'

The sense that I have is as if one does see all the time the *way* reality occurs—as having no inherent reality *really*—it's just motions—and that one is being re-trained as language continually, to think as a description of something. So, a task of writing of my period was (is) to undo one's formations, all, interior and cultural, at every instant.

Early 'terror that one is not living *then* (though living, waking at night)'—this can't be translated psychologically, or in any other way than its space. That there is no separation between *being* motion (one's mind also) and space—one has to jump out of one's skin to catch up to space. Black night, rich, is ahead, slow. So one is racing.

A man, recently responded to the phrase 'waking at night in terror that I wasn't living—when at that instant living *then*' (fear of 'not being' as not keeping inside, that is dropping out of 'motion in the writing' being the same as phenomenal motion—the writing as [is] one being alive at all). He said to me we have to accept not making all choices in life, which would be 'to be mature' (maturity is to be content). This description of 'psychological as convention' is not related to what I was describing. The pressure (urgency as terror) which I felt in *that* period of time was the effect of a sense of a 'task' that had to be done (a pressure). *One* was to change this place/the whole by a (re)writing of its minute present motion *in its* present; and has to do so without one's own ego as the mode because that would merely be duplication of *its* same pattern. 'Being as that motion' had to do with that change (the change being) limitless, entire, in the sense of open—it is related to 'seeing as being.' Language which is so delicate as in the structure of a single sentence had to reverse (to unreason) a huge weight in all space at every instant. I think this continual try, this jump was the nature of that 'early terror of not being the same as phenomenal.' The reversing of that sense which is occurring realistically—*can* be brought about conceptually, is only that, and a part of fact/phenomena, where it changes one's mind.

The conception of the poem *New Time*, for example, is to examine the mind-stuff—collapsing the mind onto the time it *is* (in); the present time as infinite and the mind being taken literally onto that same line, at every instant (as syntax—and conceptually "line" as if horizon and line of text).

A 'self' (the sense *which occurs*) isn't oneself as we construct it socially, is: as only instant of relativity.

The poem *way*, for example, is motions that are streams of double senses of interior/exterior at once, which also can be heard. If writing were oneself 'not dropping out of' its motions—then the writing would be unknown present and unknown future at once.

In *way*, motions (as syntax of the poem) are as if the inside of the outside/its infinitely random events—by the motions being the notation of (as if rendering spatially and as sound) an individual's (writer's, reader's) interior: being *their* and other's exterior actions/events (memories). The writing is thus like a sonar scan. It can only be as *that* language. That's similar to music.

The space/time of a poem is its theory of the new. In the case of *way*, real events from one's own past, so minute they can't even be remembered by oneself—changed by being in relation to the real infinity outside—are notation (the events as writing) which is *at the same time* as the outside present. *Real* outside present is always unknown and infinite, is phenomena as all time at once. It occurs by being heard.

One couldn't just propose that as writing's theory either, one would have to do it.

at 'night' any night is can't

That one can't—that night itself is outside (that) (night)
'night' 'night' burst that space. Fills it lightly. Overfills it, isn't in it. Either.

A time frame of some poets with whom I was speaking, whose writing I was reading, and meeting, sometimes being given encouragement and assistance by, friendly or contentious—in the order in which I met them, and perhaps knowing those met earlier now too:

Michael Palmer > Michael Davidson > Robert Duncan > Steve Schutzman > Kathleen Fraser > Andrei Codrescu > Lewis Warsh > Ron Silliman > Paul Vangelisti > Barrett Watten > Ronald Johnson > Rae Armantrout > Erica Hunt > Philip Whalen > Steve Benson > Carla Harryman > Bob Perelman > Alice Notley > Ted Berrigan > John Godfrey > Jim Brody > Jerome Rothenberg > Amiri Baraka > Ted Greenwald > Aaron Shurin > Clark Coolidge > Rick London > Ted Pearson > Robert Gluck > Norma Cole > Jean Day > Charles Bernstein > Bruce Andrews > Robert Creeley > Joanne Kyger > Steve Vincent > Laura Moriarty > Jerry Estrin > Beverly Dahlen > Tom Mandel > Michael McClure > Robert Grenier > Tom Raworth > Anselm Hollo > Larry Eigner > David Bromige > Kit Robinson > Lyn Hejinian > Stephen Rodefer > James Sherry > Mei-mei Berssenbrugge > Arthur Sze > Anne Waldman > Bernadette Mayer > Allen Ginsberg > David Henderson > Michael Brownstein > Alan Davies > Jackson Mac Low > Bill Berkson > Kevin Killian > Dodie Bellamy > Douglas Messerli > Norman Fischer > John Ashbery > Gail Sher > Pierre Joris > Nick Piombino > Jessica Grim > Hannah Weiner > Robin Blaser > Fanny Howe > Nathaniel Mackey > Harreyette Mullen > Claude Royet-Journoud > Rosmarie Waldrop > Dennis Phillips > Andrew Schilling > Diane Ward > Andrew Levy > Abigail Child > Peter Ganick > Ed Foster > Susan Clark > Fiona Templeton > Joan Retallack > Susan Howe > Rod Smith > Tina Darragh > Peter Inman > Jalal Toufic > Ann Lauterbach > Barbara Guest > David Shapiro >

Note: *Autobiography* was written for Gale Research, a biographical resource. I used a time scheme of a month (Oct. 14–Nov. 13, 1997) as the form. I wrote it for the $1000 payment (offered by Gale Research), as if a writing procedure: the wage for a month's writing. For example, the passage about driving to L.A. in El Niño was written on the last day of that month. It was accepted by Gale Research and held for six months before being rejected by Joyce Nakamura who said they would not publish it because: "It is too esoteric and not what our readers would expect. I mean I can appreciate the stream-of-consciousness and all—but this is going to be in *libraries!*" Later I added passages, particularly in response to helpful questions by Wesleyan editor Suzanna Tamminen.

# *Zither*

*In memory of Dan Davidson and Alma White*

Making a fictional action 'on top of' one's life's actions.

*Zither* is here partly 'commentary' on the *Autobiography* (though *Zither* was written first). I had a project of rewriting some of Shakespeare's plays: without using his characters, language, or plot. *Zither* is a rewriting of *King Lear*.

It is commentary on psyche and real-time by being a 'comic strip.' I saw a girl passing me in Golden Gate Park who had beautiful arched eyebrows like archers' bows:

The poetry and the prose are separate pairs, strands 'looking at' each other. The prose narrative is, in its splices of characters in actions, the comic strip; the boa dove is one character—she's being harassed by brownshirts, as are all the citizens; the Mayfly, another character, is a minion of the brownshirts. There is a girl with beautiful arched eyebrows who frees a horse which is being beaten by a crowd by riding the horse out of the crowd.

Note: 'his'—such as, 'his'-quiet or 'his'-fan—is 'the fact,' is or means 'there is someone else' (aware 'there is someone other').

—

A complete transformation of *Lear* is a construct of Western and Asian conceptions as the motions of the mind, only the mind *being* action or phenomena *as* writing. As to enable a state of freedom, by arriving at such an unknown shape.

that one can only be—as action—is present-time
they try to turn this as language of conversation

open
middle—to one
—at
a night
then too.

the man has no motion—as one's own mind—in his past, lying and in rotting fruit, holding out cup to one (child)—inactivity in one's present now pressed to inactive man—there—as not the child existing (then even then)—the interior is in him *and* the child *there* only—extinguishing child is anticipation

anticipation there
*is* present

As writing, the gesture in this is spatially a line in the foreground—'foreground' is one's 'mind,' one's attention as (the) present. One brings 'events' 'shreds' onto this line so that 'being in life' is either past or present or at any time. Fearing of one's or other's dying so that one raced toward it or races away—is seen in others also. It is 'to get it over with' as 'to be there' as 'to be alive.' Being alive also had at an early time such dread, such terror because of the fact of dying. Placing early events here in this simultaneous time—these events don't exist at any present (though—or having—occurred in real-time). Being in present-life occurs early. It occurs 'before' anything. There is nothing before it. Present-life 'now' is what is 'early'—it is in fact utterly free

Extended texts which can articulate one's early interior as *being* the 'outside' culture in conflict, and being at the same time separate from its social formation, are an investigation of the action of one's 'mind,' which itself is apprehension only as that phenomena (action of seeing) there.

sail

only

The inner is articulated as the outer being its movement, by itself only so that is never power
The intention of the shape as thought created is to change perspective (as being itself a thought), occurring as the specific ground (that shape)

spring is in

some—a—life—in
present

By the activity being separated from the language and going on at the same time
activity is the only community.


Noticing that someone is seeing one as sustaining men who being only in custom are not them.
They're not there. View of sustaining them is her, in some other being eliminated for them.

as for me later actual land in coming down in the plane at S.F.

physical blackness of land *created* by [one's] vulnerability—to stupidity—is letting it alone

Separation of physical motions and articulation create an experience of 'foreknowledge.'
'Plots as actions' stem from each other here as if arising by their own occurrence without being tracked beforehand.

which may be—only in the present—man's

— black humps—mountain's

night


which doesn't weigh—mountain's

man's lying on side's night


where they are. mountains


    Someone described this sense of action in a text (in which "Every-
thing occurs out ahead") as being his own experiencing as reader:
"<u>Often</u> feeling <u>joy</u> participating in speedy reading of it / <u>with</u> it—enthu-
siasm of (dreamy) disbelief/belief, that 'life' can really transpire, actual—
remember waking up to certain days when very young, like this, in pure
anticipation ('foreknowledge') that what will happen will be wonderful—
<u>what will happen next</u>?—<u>no matter what</u>."

    woman looks like cheetah—her eyes
    from one being within train—jumps—one—is

    The sense of "no matter what" is important; the events of history are
the 'experience' of happiness, or can only be felt as that (in this; my in-
tention is to create that surface, which is experienced as this).

                  playing zither in spring present—and
                  it's not spring yet—no child
                  here

The train cars in which in one as a child packed in intense heat of night or day, yellow cracked vast ground on which white cattle straggle, the people tearing at the sides of the train when it would come into the station, as there was a famine, are as past or not memory in the present. zither ocean

—how—
could—there—be

— carcasses—anywhere
— the thought—is one

Detachment of the action—imitation as this as if the mental shape or anticipation of running, out ahead—or action of running behind (where there is only the present yet there is as if subliminal sense of events which actually occurred, not repressed),—so it is 'as' thought; and the activity detaching 'sole,' neither past nor present as memory, is reading which is 'foreknowledge' as its action (reading) *per se*.

within—hair-pin formation—as dawn—voluptuous
*'him'*

People running beside the trains begging—have to be returned to— as the happiness of the child there. One now.

Resistance is therefore delineation as mimicry—one—which is action separated from it there.

They think it's resistance in one, but it is the action—there, separated.

and mightn't not be *only* there
can't be imposing actions—on one

So that the kid (then) to return there as to happiness, struggles to do so, wants to stowaway on freighters. *At that time* detaches it and is in action now—that the present *be* (is) sole (there).

One is going to have to dismantle all minute events—in one—as being out there [in the adult oneself], that being imperialism only in a child 'there' 'one' as one *now*.

We have no relation to the past therefore, as it being 'before' [ahead of] oneself. The increasing obfuscation [social] of any ground of observation is outdone by the child/oneself to be a ground.

'Our perspective' or conceptualizing is being eliminated so one's eliminating one's perspective is not secret action, inner, it is action that dismantled existing

One other event occurs—in one.

The relation of oneself to events of the past, and to history—are [rendered] as if 'history,' as if it is one [which is 'imperialism' *per se*, there are no words this is word substitution]


to eliminate the ground of poetry, it has become scrutiny


man in rowboat falling—no
present or child

One's return to the place of action—which is happiness (of kid, there)—occurs by observing one's appearance in 'physical' motions; our convention of being separated here is 'foreknowledge.'

To say that this is about being women—rather than being men when one isn't—is to deny one's [occurring as an act] here—one's actions. here—only.

I want to create an extremely simple surface, in which happiness is 'felt'—*because* it doesn't exist here, in living being conceptualization.

to enter
in the middle

or side—anywhere

in life

    The simple surface as solely detached action out ahead is expressed in
its separation, and in the sense of this simple surface going on 'after' as
well.
    It's regarded as pretentious and without social elevation too.
    'I have but slenderly known myself' and so I repeat. Knowing oneself
only slenderly is a certain action.

    flagged whales—present—died—'there'—as a state or condition, a
place
    no more—free—one had to stowaway 'to them' who're lying in
garbage—one (as child)—['their' as adults]—at that present.

a future can

be separate

    —one has no other
existence
    the forest

    past is.—separate—one is the same as they
    but it's that there wasn't—authority—for anyone—by itself only so
that is never power
    Difficulty breathing now—cattle wave freighter in thought

    'as' child—interested in submarines. Cattle are on billows of grass.
    reactionaries—bearing hatefully—on one—at party—is happy from
one's going after one for whom one cares
    happy for caring
    one doesn't care for these.

                              outside
                              cattle

                              freighters
                              are

                              in night—one

            dusk's freighters
cattle
            [night not being so—conjecture]
are also birds—[as the conjecture and in them *per se*]
*Separate to the side—continuous—one's*

and                                          a—it's not
refugees—are in              — in —
    —the middle—with                one—outside shape
[famine]—first                — hasn't that space
                                        ahead in one—[is]


    to walk
in
an unstable and ungoverned country
          array [of] —
armed factions                              — to one side
are still—fighting          *outside*
                              [one's breathing]


                              shape, *as shape*, is on the side
                              [as it—at all]


                              one's
                              breathing has to
                                    realign—*to*—it
                              can't—[yet]

the
few trickling—back in
—said [they're]
—dying
of thirst dysentery in panicked

flight

their—refugees
—space—outside—one's
breathing
then
being inside—the *'outside'*

anticipated first, not known before

being heard *when* it hasn't been
heard
first—one

yet—they [factions]
*want* starving
waiting to feed
ends—them [refugees]

breathing—is
—in—outside—one's
—outside shape
has
forgotten

—[yet]

many—left behind—outside breathing—
dying.
one's not breathing *in* events
either

[*one is breathing 'in' events*]


       hearing *before* it is
heard

       [occurring]
       isn't one's interior

—or anticipation

       *five hundred thousand shown*
       *walking on field*
one's [a] 'shape'
—not being
   —either—the present

or people [convention] [one]
in—a life—
    early
*is* present
     — '*in*'


### Life of the Mayfly


   Whereas carrying the nuts swaddled in the robes, as if sandbags which they haul in the robes on the side of the black mounds at night— one woman caters as assuming the nuts in robes is removed from others even—and *office* has respect 'only,' not even apprehension
   black mounds being night—lines of people carrying coal on the black mounds—mounds as mountains at night—*are*.

   A tiny figure in the immense darkness, the nuts in robes dragging the night—sandbag, plummets under the moon, into the arms of the standing figure

   (as tiny child on playing field, with no thin moon, thinks where ball will come, moving there, it plops into the child's arms) yet the figure, with that other immense nuts in robes weighing in the moving liquid sky—has not anticipated

There is no activity but community—what activity *is*—one is by one-self—and they're hauling the sand bags with the view that nuts in robes is office (as if that were merit *per se*) 'alone.' 'Only.' Not 'one.'

The dress light in it of woman seated at tea—outside—not in my experience as act—how?—so the sensation of happiness
beginning from this point—how?

Mocking as such—being at present. And as being at present has no authority.
The overweening sack mocking, which is authority itself, and in having one's sandbags dragged.
The experience of being mocked from in reality and their being in that. as if it were significant that one were mocked, that is, anyone
having to explode, detonate, power—because that is oneself
—real authority outside, of others

it is that not imposed

outside—one—one entirely different from the conflict occurring

conflict not occurring in silence or night—being re-delineated to occur in one
transitions are it's being missed, to have occurred but not now
nothing now is blindness occupants emerging—not REM, event in spring

She characteristically makes suffering to one as not arising from thought and assuming office is in apprehension as being it—apprehension as no-thought causing and intolerant
unconscious as free-floating—aggression that is not 'planned out' or seen—what is action never seen by the one in action?
The city is in a brown haze.

the other not having authority crushes people jeered by him

so the other is to have no authority ever as the delicate means of those people in camps, imported labor, not being crushed?

no authority in one *is* ignorance—and being only in the most fragile place

                          edge has

                          sail

one's interior fighting—is conventionality—as reasserting separation of one and dawn—in people's oppression

dawn is.—not now—. yet torture of one's inner fighting to realign—outside

seeking outside—customs—as the means to *not* realign one

The Mayfly hauling the blonde sandbags in a dither, state of force moving suction in reverse, makes flip remarks to the other—that one sees 'those people' [who are being curtailed] are authoritarian *in fact* (that is, *they* are that).

go in
in

the middle
or—a side

in

trajectory is in the middle

The sacks hanging, emaciated people are crawling on coal mounds—this is in a city (the same time, in different places).

People in the city wade [at the same time].

freighter zither

is

*In order to be seated the viewers have to walk*

There's a shadow of the words that shimmers. A samurai comes up in the grass.

Huge variegated hairy blotched moths hit on the light outside.

—

The other is ushered into a plush office in spring.

Woman's throat a banded dove's neck heaving in speaking, as if she were a boa swallowing what is immense, speaks as the dove's plump breast-throat heaves in its band.

The other is to be hired to protect the dove, to be the guard of the non-celebrity.

The layers, lids in folds of the heaving boa dove bulging above the band also bug as does the throat.

The throat bugging is a swell, a breast.

Bellicose without intentionality.

Over here. *Man seated at a café table outside, gesticulating to signal, as if for a cabby, says* Over here, over here.

The heaving boa dove bulging at the constraint on the bugging neck is inside. There's a conflict for attention (between boa dove and unknown man at café table—for the other).
Maintains wants errands on the corner—then it will be night.

The soft dark sides of the horse lying being kicked in the long grass with their coming through the sea of grass from all sides
to hold too much

The soft dark rolling sides-cage of curled horse lying—mounds in grass
They're (their) kicking in at the sides

> train on parch cracks
> is freighter—at night

A man, the interior nature of muscular dove—cage—one stretches out on the throat-breast raking it, the base of it while his dove moves—remaining soaked
one

> not changing
> by
> the middle—being
> in
>
> one—or side is
> one is that

He applies his brilliant gentle mind to the fact in the grass. The kicking people in long grass yet being a tyrant one is respected *per se.* for that.
This is not the movement in the grass.
Nor is their movement zither—we had a zither, as children; there is freighter
they are themselves *in fact*
Hemmed in by the long spears, the other in the middle—spears through grass, the people holding them on the other ends on all sides—the other is hemmed pricking as spear-punctures that are on her sides.
One first—the other does—runs in before (before them being there)—

One is running out—something occurs *then*, when one is running

not anticipating, as in happiness—running out—before is happy,
something occurring does not change that then. experiencing being
happy is in the present, that it *will* be. (*Is* in the future then, at the same
time.)

as the middle—of a conflict—in one then being.

is there not being authority—
is shape—the man knows this—
*loves*—as what his shape *is*.

At the drug store
the mayfly has layers of transparent webbed wings like a dragonfly's
veins yet rungs of them on her sides—Man O War—swells on which the
jell-eggs are floated
the eyes of the eggs, she is blind yet not really
whorl—the other is running past her—by placing her belly on the
plate-glass of a shop window and urinating the eggs as the other runs by.
They float.

came down in entire life span outside

One runs in front first—but the other had got there—first is vast
streaming sloughed off of jell-eggs in the blue.
[These are comic strips—invented as one goes along, so are from
one's mind as ahead and behind it at the same time.]

there's no authority is
its
[early/at] time—he *loves*—'*as*'—
'*in*' time]

'to know oneself only slenderly'—man nearly translucent lying in sea
of rotting fruit on street of port holding out cup, on glazed eyes not car-
ing, as others are the same, starving—walking in amidst them, 'as'
child—one—from freighter, one has to do this

sensation of being happy as foreknowledge is out there, while entwined with coming in at port and as present [at this time now] not dependent on this event

        *is* the action—not
the memory—the action counts
                           man in rowboat past
                           in present
the event, of translucent man lying starving—and but slenderly knowing oneself always (which is before this, before the man takes his life)—are the same
    [action occurring. This was begun for Dan Davidson, died from suicide in 1996.]

    Two times that are placed together are joined—by but slenderly knowing myself

    the event is *not* myself.
    and 'obtuse about people really' related to other things, a tendency

    Not by unconscious association, but by the event not being oneself—at all; because all that is known of the events is known at present; can't be known further; and besides, it did occur

                  has no weight

    This particular event, of the starving man, have to have foreknowledge at the time—and there isn't any—can't be, different from cognitive so that's active.

    an event—is to be by itself—by one but slenderly knowing oneself.
[rewriting *Lear* as a form]
    being naive about people's actions now. as a tendency

                past
                in present—isn't dependent there

    the sensation in one of being happy, as foreknowledge then—the man takes his life (now) *when* the man lying starving (the two placed on the same time)—oneself [who's adult] to be the actual child *then* at present

    [young then wanting] to get back—[conceived now] to past wanting stowing away on freighters—is to get to man *at present* starving *then* 'in future'—so as no-authority. to dissolve events—but they *have* dis-solved—*as* (what's) foreknowledge

*and*

subservience required or one not to be known by him (who is requir-ing it)—also (required from the man who'd taken his life)—given noth-ing from 'the one requiring subservience' except to do that—by just some other
could be any one

falling out—through the ocean—so there's no existing present.
the present is sole, the youth (oneself) then wanting stowing away on freighter—to return
if there is no society [it is in future there, there is none]

subservience of some to some other here who asks from anyone ac-tion of subservience where there is no sense to it, to giving it, other than requiring it.

"There's no use talking about anything serious."—"Why not?"—"Because what's the use?, we don't *know* anything serious.
Cattle standing on the deep waves—are indigo then—cowboys (one) herd them, one is asked what one wants to be
they push in sides—is—without moving in one herds them

the brownshirt man holds out his hand, to eat in it in the water and the other man does not do so by but slenderly knowing himself.
limited knowledge and no value by people—*cattle move on the people in water.*

Someone else.
weight of his having taken his life—it is fall—soon freezing dawn
is cattle


herding cowboy (one) kicking the cattle forward as many of them are walking on the deep ocean; in which they are not affected, they don't move, by being kicked by one yet wouldn't be moving there—*remove anticipating as foreknowledge is just there*

early—women-cattle incarcerated below deck
—of ship—while one walked
　　—child
walks—people's present—
　　separated intellect feeling—'as' hierarchy
'their'—'to' violate hearing-dawn existing


'to' violate hearing 'as' dawn 'in'
existing—is ship's-ocean
　　night—no mediation—yet faculty being that itself
freighter's action's-not-one

base's-hierarchy unmediated

　　not being in action—which it is, women-cattle
below deck
　　—of ship—in occurrence is 'there'
'at the time' also—is only [a] dawn's-action


['for them'] as being 'in' dawn's-action
of their occurrence [only]


　　isn't in any actions—as no one—
not having occurred—yet [or
　　it isn't itself] ever—as
its being

The brownshirt has throttled the dreamy boa dove and is girdling the banded breast-throat which hums bugging.

Above and below the banded breast-throat gurgles the boa dove dainty. The hum being inside the heaving fat coils bugging are on the outside softly flexing—in the fist.

Brownshirt's fist slowly clutches. Cognition arises in his fist.

I want you to drop your little load like a donkey. *Suddenly a bag of dung falls from brownshirt's rear.*

Nothing is said. Boa dove appears embarrassed.

Brownshirts in clandestine activity here selling crack in the inner cities of their own people to finance a foreign war are on the street during the moon's eclipse separated in the light film—their colostomy bags shone like humps on their backs.

one in eclipse shines—is in inner city—selling—*one can exist 'at' the time*

The other approaches boa dove and a brownshirt who is slapping the dove who ruffled splats on wall backward
and Other holds his fist, simply holds it softly
shrugs the ripple of the colostomy bag hump in the watery air

Nothing is said. To them gliding humps.

The next time the mayfly is seen she's wearing Chador, the black robes and veil forced *here* on women
who is a ding-bat winging with her head screwed on backward
as the women are forced into ditches
the spring swims
Mayfly liked—life—has—a radio program in the war—telling women they have to be women to lead a woman's life. ("They have to lead a woman's life to be women.")

The account of events as 'history' is mechanical, rendering being-time as separate, for it to be separated as not real
the desperate effort to render one as coexistent with 'events' is to be separate
*why be separate even? let it slip and we're not inside*

is itself that experience recurring—the description of which realigns by cognition itself. One has to disorient it outside.

Meeting—her head screwed on backward speaks into the wake in the watery air only—as if she were driving a roadster.

Her black pinned fans, the brownshirt throttles boa dove and a man walking.

The nature of power *itself* being their not caring if they are 'accurate'—*or* seen as that—to anything—*per se*.

[*no one* taking theirs to be fact not mattering] [to them]

so one's mimicking them—occurs—separately—'then'

'*as*':—black humps mountains—then '*as*'

people crawling on coal—mountains' night—does

    in clarity
    being 'no' friendship
[in the time]
    —his (some one's) *perversity*—
*is* free
    as *lack of 'clarity'*

*His perversity doing nothing is not what they say is clarity*
*italics is print only—joy*

*it has to be from anon. reverse*
    herd
    too—[throwing]
    at black
    night
    'there'

buttocks cracked running in the grass night
horse

buttocks cracked at dawn in grass black night [are] isolated

buttocks cracked pair on banded [evening] night [are] isolated

buttocks cracked pair on banded [evening] neck-dawn—bug. [bugging]

[lying in the grass]

too.—pair. dawn.

additionally rim evening—isn't—
in existence

    A woman doesn't value others in guiding converse of theirs, one—
[so—evening isn't in existence]—they're to play only. in a certain way.
doesn't receive new input as conversation doesn't take place and is
guided—conversation can't be guided

it is all there is

    dual is the nerve in one's arm—*but* within.
    not as a child.

    one can't say anything—as it is conventionality—at all
    any one to jump through only—as not to do so is [one]
    one goes backward in night and utterly free—as in many (there are)
or any nights (outside)

    inexperience itself is anticipation
    hadn't been in a forest forward on one's one-wheel cycle—at all—
and—thin as if half—disk light wallow on rim of sky and horizon's line
    not having a line and disk-sphere—at all

the one-[wheel cycle at night

in 'center' (?) at night, too (?)


learns on the one-wheel cycle forward—?—
is night?

never being there *before*

    Lear is the viewer. One might even loosen this faculty (sensual as exterior/interior at once) of apprehension further from one's stream. (*Zither* is the rewriting of *King Lear* as Kurasawa's *Ran*—which doesn't have this in it)


A little white owl springs up gliding toward one

the girl with eyebrows curved like bows follows it into the plumed grass
the moon or sun resting on the plumed grass, both then

walk on plumed grass

horse

    down crowds coming in from the long plumes eyebrows arch following phosphorescent owl gliding in

    in fireflies crowds sides running on its sides

    crowds running on its sides wallows on black grass

    crowds wallow eyebrows on moon-edged horse-blackness

    crowds wallow grass horse gliding moon

    eyebrows arching through grass wallow moon

    eyebrows wallow crowd on the horse

    the man at the cafe outside in the light appears to be wearing magpie's glistening black feathers gliding blackness
    crowd comes in plumed grass to little white owl

    head in blackness and running legs in plumed grass

seated roils in sun and moon both then on half-plumed wall-grass
crowd in sun and moon both then wallows on wall-plumes and seated
to the side the half

horse
alone walking beside man who's seated at cafe in glistening black wall
to plumed grass in crowd


I saw this film (*I The Worst of All*)—of a Mexican cloistered nun in
time of the Inquisition, poet who thought voluptuously given up then to
it at early time [thought is experienced in conversation as slow time in
the film]—later recanting [agreeing in the Inquisition] before dying in
the plague.

The boa dove has hired the detective to protect her from the brown
shirts, who are putting peoples' furniture in trucks. The people are liv-
ing out on the streets already.

The Mayfly flits by a parade of brownshirts, walking beside them—
the other seated at a café. It's evening, a parade in evening.

longing for cabs

                    *in*experienc*ed*—is—future

recanting that she had been night
*weighs*—living as a pagan in the convent—'*in*' breath's dusk

one's existing-dusk

that is in present
yet death isn't paired

we had a zither
(children

) which we couldn't play

not knowing how

[not related to now in
dying]


zither "why"

communicating

freighters

sea at night

hurl—in the middle—or

midst [doesn't have to be the middle]—some

in one's life—with what?

[with what?]

going at it with cockiness won't do it—as 'not' one—however being
seen as going forward only

too. forward can be humility?

don't know
what's *then*

Some people belly-up—to show submission, the soft and sweet spar-
row bellying-up—so that they will not charge and then tear her.
Humility—to lead them. to placate

by placated

But some other cannot belly-up—as it is not allowed for anyone in conception, for one—it's irrelevant
so they charge and tear at her and others continually—only.

a separation occurs

'One' has an interiority there—that is neither one nor aggression. So does humility in the one.

colostomy bags ripple, humps on the men walking

yet that placates them—humps of the colostomy bags floating. But it is toward people but isn't people.

starving man is first—
early freedom—is now only

It isn't astute so it's giving up on observation.

I have no idea what this has to do with dying. Closure of early free-dom in width—*isn't*
.interiority—is not one—ocean mid in—it to rowed being—by the whales [yet who floated harpooned]
'not' aiming for intellectual clarity—so people value him—
'leading'—jumps—

Bongo was a young bear in the Disney film who in the circus train wreck at night enters [on one-wheel cycle] into forest
he goes by—Bongo in forest flits then—long low guttering then oc-curs—rim—yet [and] his black train

Bongo's train
observe

one


rim—outside breathing

they say they have *no* narrative outside

that are
sensual moves are *one's* narrative

and they have none. is [*their*] power
[not event]
occurs 'there'



a breath goes in beach

Long flat beach to ocean's edge—breath gets into the flat beach of
night, or within.
The night is within the breath. There.
Night 'in' stevedores, 'the' 'are' blooms—[on the outside]—for two
people remember that same 'event'

Didn't think that people would be as they really indicated they were

not basing it on the child—and the child perceiving what occurs is
not based on authority—despairing as it is not capable

—as freedom in rickshaws
early freedom

ocean ball—in future span sky [is in]—too at all one's—
Two—starting out in rickshaws—no supervision then in the
city

early freedom—leading to blossomed spring
separation—as one—leading to bud

—as no authority existing at all is only—so it's not itself even—
children insulted in school racially—too there—early freedom

                nothing is based
                on anything

One exists now on only past (present) as 'nothing' (as that being in
fact, events—since placing the past at present *is* dissolved)

Humiliating children regarding their race until they stamped and
screamed.

then they did also, the adults got out of the way. the realignment by
present-adult didn't work. we're not. past.

to change. the past. 'at' present. *no need.*

She dotes on everything that has balls—to sustain them, fanning
their ego, so there cannot be love, that is despair—if one doesn't have
balls though one is not sustained

                by anything

Look get this straight, I dote on everything that has balls.

Everyone begins writing in in letters, Look, she dotes on everything
that has balls, meaning favorably of that.

*[Mayfly seated at café table still holds swathed balls and with her glistening
sails pinned wide black fans outside: Fact in occurrence (past)—is in one's physi-
cal frame—too, dawn.]*

*Then the ballooned fans turn red in the black sun.*

The load is so great one'll have to be carried off to the loony bin and
*will* here sustain one—

                here we're
                pretending

I think we should get to utter level of infant [an inner track of de-
spair]—has something to do with dying one isn't now that's it—but that
really—as infantile [thin track, line], humps of the colostomy bags on
brownshirts them gliding to one and one hits them swatting with news-
paper to have them continue gliding
say how.


moving one's hands [their] constantly speaking and then moving
them at night-voluptuous [is]—*when*

sleep
occurs—one—physical pairs 'singly'

black humps mountains there.


     tiny child [one] thinks—seeing
—people laboring on road
    with tiny bound bird's feet
       of upper class—that
one 'has to' seek 'enlightenment' must *then*

One cannot tell a separation between them with humps gliding and
their pretending. One's pretending and theirs are so similar as simply
pretending—how are we going to be an infant without being infant?

*demystify life—so one can do it.*


saw curled woman on motorcycle
another waiting for her—on span ahead

—separated from one's—thorax, there

(not) breathing at all—bursting—breathing there

thorax black in shining blue wide
thin—place—of *their* moving

then one's thorax loosened laughs in space
boy on skateboard speeding downhill—the thorax opens—one's

one's—black thorax in pelting rain opens
[separately] *slow*

The ice-floes—seals flipping in blackness—begin to break up, yet before is one, or is when one leaves—the colostomy bags waver in the wind. I've forgotten the news. I disturbed myself.

Ice on wind people at night wading in the freezing drift and city immediately (as eclipse) [at the same time]

> put future nights
> only—just

that one is an outcaste (disliked) for sticking a spear into goose in sedan chair.—the blood trickling out, yet her later getting out so the shaft doesn't seem to have penetrated her (to the hilt)—infantile but on a rim of her awareness
the clarity of the infantile to such a degree as to really be infant—and not sustained—people not sustaining such

Say how. We don't value that. He won't speak to me from my good aspects and one swatting the passing figure humped with a newspaper, one time
what is effective isn't anything
as is one's—as infant, now—sticking spear into side of sedan chair

But there can't be any recognition of not able to try

[the others slap each other as affection
in forest—one slaps him
the 'center' being *them*—always]


he, valued for authority as such, not speaking as to show that, have
that—one can't separate as that is one

one's obsession—one doesn't exist any more—strike him only [one
cannot behave in this manner—is inner}—infant before (is what occurs)

gravel as unsustained lucidity that's pre-experience—what does this
have to do with someone else dying?
he some one only thinks in one's ego is to sustain his acts—so one is
nothing

an infantile without action emerged in one as being in other people,
innocent really, kind others encountered, by chance.
Saw some.
Infant—thin.

Someone else pretends to sustain males—to sustain herself only—so
there is an unsustained world—*despair*—with no love, a specific action
as one *has* love—in fact

a prior ghost of oneself—that's torture—that isn't one but a stand-in
apparition where one isn't existing now—neither one nor the apparition
is a representation
missing dawn—in intensity—though illumined line in wide space
jumped not anyone or dawn—at all.

one could do from reverse of seeing the dawn from next day—not
anyone—
child and one are not parted—anywhere—the sensation of happiness
before—
the stand-in apparition is neither—nor is dawn—
An emotion, or a relation between two others, changes entire mass
continuum outside. This can be perceived in sound.

the thorax can't relax to breathe in despair jumped dawn in one—
wide—one can't exist so apparition occurs—
yet precedes dawn—

no thorax—is [when dawn]

breathing at dawn illumined line


can't base it on an event, say of man falling from rowboat in whales—
that at or occurring to the side

one anticipating as they can't be seen, they glide by the humps on
them flashing in the bright, infantile, and a spear pops one of the colos-
tomy humps—it flashes writhing

after
it

*They go after it.* I've been breathing in my neck an eclipse

one is not in
it

One is the same as others—in forest
resistance to any—formation—in life—at all
customs are inherently interior.

love, secret while the relation yet in public visible—by ones being separate from public—the man with oneself separate moves visible.

he hasn't the same relation to those who are seen out in public while he moves visible there.


bugged boa dove out ahead of brownshirt—squeezed out of fist—others—kicked horse in grass at night—one
by café
seated customer saying Over here. still there at night. again—which is not existing—is voluptuous

Ocean at night but looked at at past event hurl [with what?]
Present bears no resemblance to the present-past

the other here is the ornery self, disliked in one separates—who is to protect—boa dove being girdled before one—inside by café, moon—the horse in the long grass at night, sensation of happiness begin at this point—without motivation

one is not aligned—*despair*—even at the end of one's life (a woman at death now)

some one action is night [is 'not occurring' also]

*is* intellect—of one's breath alive 'at' night—it is—speaking to bud
—[that *had* (blossomed)]
a lack of rigorous thought being brought to anything
one [has to]

hierarchy-fakery in no thought analysis in itself
this does not occur in bud, which is before [at the same time]
people view hierarchy as 'brilliant'

one state of sleep meets in prior state of sleep—land in deep black outside
the land is deep black—one
at the same time

one sleep episode—[and] there is no other prior sleep there—

grey voluminous billow sky—[and] black land [a different time], one
on curve of outside land in deep black there—only.
half-cracked bud reached—past—outside—at all

jumped [as if outside state of sleep]—while it was existing—one exist-
ing 'there' at the same physical line, of land in deep black outside—too

a flight of bridge—in sky—*then* can't breathe

'at'—woman is curled on motorcycle—on span

*when*
future-another curled on motorcycle waiting ahead

—so—outside—then one's thorax loosened laughs in space

sensation of happiness then [past]—future—black tulip,
which is breathing—has nothing to do with it being in the future

*Bongo*

some life—in—present—'causes'—spring?—black tulip, which is
breathing—on one's one-wheel cycle—in—future-past—the forest
zither

spring—in them—one's—configuration—of only knowing—oneself
slightly—as *being*—events—is—something—else—occurring—there

walking—could go before—no oppression of separation—there it-
self—seeking customs—in—[and before]—a—life

put—in one—in a long—span—one's—black—night—in—center—
(or somewhere)—in that [the] life—span—itself—one's interior—aligned
by people there—yet night—


put in one—then—people's aligning—as one's interior—present—
is—alone—in past—span—present—black nights—there
someone—else's—aligning—present then—one's—a present—black
—there


who—anyone—dropping dusk—one

they—as—being—one's interior—space as black night—and—lit
day—put—in one—there


dropping dusk—

[people's 'sound' *as evening first*


the [evening] [dusk] first in their

—there—black—evening

crowd before—
between them silent forest—existing—one

—one's interior [as them—only]—is—evening—night—there
this isn't people—ocean drops lit beach—people—do cart-wheels—
there. striated lit clouds—some—more do cart-wheels—there—again.

[not going to get closer—one's—to separation]

they're not inner—no oppression of separation—there—then—[at
present]—[in them]

—has to do [with]: having to live here—and therefore one is not ca-
pable—anyone.

people starving dying—*as*—fact—is not capable—there either.


woman with her children—[is]—picking corn on stalks by hot lit
road—this would be a memory (as if theirs) or won't (of hers?)—even
be—there.
as if seeing her is one's mother—there—with one—[and] it isn't.
one being [now] not child—not dependent on one as child—there.
[and doesn't want authority]—anywhere
[—then—one is not capable—anyone]



             the forest isn't [   ]—              [
        nothing's [   ]          / extinction]

Pain (of child) of a lightning prong sent in it. Whang. as it is the first time (only occurrence) of its burning out the one's interior wires.

The lightning (a bolt) having blasted out its interior, that is in silence, in intense conflict anyway.

one's inner is not—yet an intense conflict, a silent hair-pin formation which is a pair, destroys and is [present]—

it has to continue being destroyed [one] in order to not be there [in silence]—or in order to be *'any'* present—and there being an intense conflict. *then*. spring.

this is fact in occurrence in one's physical frame—not duplication of inner motions *outside*, but may *be* in those—is. too.

Of course at that age one had never heard of *anything*. Nothing, and this was happening. Could be *spring*. It *is*.

'Now.'

*at night—'at'—night*

—and seeing that that culture inscribes such—a spatial—like throwing—is *spring night—in summer—there—one [yet silent paired with no conflict]*

in dawn—there is nothing outside—
early child—in—is—
no silent pair, i.e. paired 'there'

it's—only
this—shape

is there not being authority—is shape

moon [on base]—is where—horse running on its back in long grass night

*'on' night 'at' night* is *also*.

—not silent hair-pin—dawn

silent dawn—*before*—people crawling lines carrying coal—
[and] there—is the same silent space—?—night [one]

"Moving the goal post"

I kept losing my bearings—because the eye drifting away—is it

The thrashing-bosom above the banded throbbing coil is ahead in the dusk's dawn—a space that is not known—her neck in the fist of the man humped colostomy bag on him.

The action is in that space, transgresses there

(*Mayfly holds up hoop through which Other jumps once, occurring before she says "I forgot"*): There isn't a reason why one other could be protected more than some other—yet one is to protect that one, as the action outside.

Someone (else) as her conversation only holding up a hoop—I forgot—I forgot to jump through, and so she hates me.

The forest having no volition as not dawn yet

the men humped colostomy bags on them tearing after others are in quiet space—or the man starving lying in rotting rinds

as swims humped man the colostomy bag wavering in sea of moon, the moon's hanging in a huge protrution (sic)—and men floating on their colostomy bags fin

the woman a mayfly then comes to the night coming to the charged thick plumed grass as choked action as *being* night rather than *it* coming to one

a movement which *they think* is resistance. A movement has no independent existence *per se*.

An anonymous worker—stretched as if an amber insect or seen between the arms of an amber desert machine—working on the desert where there are no other people—and stretched thinly webbed from the constant work he is only work (*per se*) in the desert by the huge drill or machine stretched on the filmy surface—no other people there.

The desert or sand-storms unseen while he's working or momentarily seen 'through' him stretched on or between the prongs of the machine's horizon as its-desert outside (the desert's horizon), him having leapt there?

One sees him, not looking, as the hanging desert him on the

mounted machine almost transparent. He's an amber moth hitting—on the desert, almost a slingshot
It is not him in reverse.

Rubbing liniment on the cheeks—pressed dawn is.
The man rubbing liniment on one's cheeks the muscles rippling—inky air standing—held still, by there being the actions only—one's is-before
One's thigh trembling is put forth in the desert no blooms anywhere.
Holds the right leg stretched flexing and slaps the buttocks to run hardly moving.
Buttocks inky waking.
*They're persecuting the bookworm.*

May, herself a tiger with the multi-veined, vein-rippled side, has dug trenches covering these with boughs so that the other out, a twig snapping, hurls drops into the deep trench except holding on to a bough of a tree.
The panting striped sides wall-sides of the tiger walls wallow as it leaps perched on a ledge.

One's drinking night—not from people. Humped figure sucking over a crumpled form is seen [in headlights hump of colostomy bag] and rises slightly-staggering up running away.]

Others bulging bug on the moon then bulging on brown hill 'by' factories.
The horse in the high plumes gallops on its back in black, sighs, the brown hill a dove.

the tiger-wall perched leapt there wall-sides swiveling at the side wallowing wall-sides hanging as leapt are 'at' moth at night's night

wallowing wall-sides leapt on boughed ledge

While hanging on bough nothing comes to mind.
Girl appears running arms arch at hip parting and a ball hurls out dips baseball hurtling to other who's hanging by tree's bow girl runs on.
tree bough sky dropped waiting at wall-sides hanging lunge with a limb out in sky
city

transgresses in space—at night in the city saw the police have one fellow down on the sidewalk a foot on his neck four police cars for one man.

None is interior or outside, yet slightly aside from both and single

that isn't isolation or the excitement of the doves brushing by him dragging

the boa dove as if bursting a gullet speaking anyway

one has no others to do this yet there is a space one sees one. one has no employees then the moon bursts the high plumes of grass. the moon bursts the grass sea at the horse. there is no action the moon bouncing on flattened indigo is isolating man flapping black glistening pinched fans—behind horse—

not there. gullet has moon in it yet not burst grass plumes wall aside floating itself breathing on one's neck

The tiger, seen as an apparition itself. Man seated at café says Over here, Over here as if viewer were a waiter in rain.

At the side is rain. At the side at night. Waiter comes to him with food in the sea of rain.

action is cracked or
half
    —nothing or one
being as action—first—
    one isn't outside 'it' either—so
it can't be itself

One collapses one-as-present in dusk's-dawn, a phenomenal space

One's-as-present is different, which can't be enacted [will be, occurring]

White owl shoots forward ahead on girl with the dark arched eye-
brows as slaps buttocks on moon's base to run in the beating crowd

the horse starts from crowd while arched eyebrows slap horse's but-
tocks in crowd

coming straight forward arched eyebrows on crowd through it wal-
lows at the night's crowd's sides

her left thigh comes forward gently in the crowd on buttocks of horse

horse rolls running neck at night crowd in grass—in dusk's-dawn

one having no volition as not dawn in that space—or there being
dusk on crowd

dangling black night thigh


~~


trees can't be translated—'in'

elation—jump—
rain

—is 'from' trees—'in'


~~


trees—on—red rain—not 'to'
them (rain)

the trees are 'to' one
opened trees' fan—with none—in it—there [their]—trees


~~

their 'to'—
one's—interior fan

black trees—'in'—he 'loves'

—[and] one's trees-fan—there's

there—trees—'on' red rain—the


~~


then—his / one—[occurs before]—there
in existence is trees-fan

'on'
one red-rain—just one

the

~~


'the'—is fan—'before'

red-rain—[not one—or 'in']—'there'

[[and]


~~

one isn't 'in'
trees—forest—

(one's) trees-fan is in rain
one

       'so' red-rain is—then 'the'

~~




he—as not trees-fan
      red

too

there


~~


     of the reactionaries—'some' others—

     —the.

     forest. exists

     'on' fan—not one's—'the'

~~

     now

     —rain falling—it's not red—he

—isn't in space of rain [and dawn? or him

one him there trees-fan too [so is fan] there's—

     too

[fan is huge]

~~

fans-forest. there

yet
'the'.
outer-fan—there is no outer fan—is

his

~~




        'reverse grace'
and fans-forest

blackening fan—is wind

one's—as outside walking
[his]



~~




        —to
notice
        'reverse grace'—him—'love'

early fan
outer walking

early


~~

        his
—walking on trees

—one—[and]—he—loves—[in the middle]
        his
—walking on trees

'at'

red-rain's fan—early
—and—'in' night


~~


        his
planks as dawn [heart's valve—rungs]—goes on
        opened so people's leaving camps
at night
people's tendons being hacked in many—in
        along—
in planks [his—dawn] leaps one him their—to side

        night
        base—there is no base


~~

breaks past rungs while in their middle—
dawn's
    his—people's—fleeing camps—one's
bursting—'in' it—separate—is—on his

    his quiet's
[[his] 'heart's'—valve] burst 'on'—a—dawn time—one's


~~


    his quiet's
people fleeing
rungs' planks

    his one's rungs
trees' red-rain's planks


~~


    —one's [mother]—jumps—dusk bars
    [of train]—crossing 'comes forward'
to—
    ding—is dusk—people starving early—her
    as jumps rung—any—additional-
    ly—only

~~

one's [father]—the fact 'as'—reverse grace
will—be—dawn's

[too]
[and] people starving early—will be 'on'—'is'
his

not even additionally


~~


—his [other man's]—people starving
—being hit—is 'on'

one's night—night—additional-
ly

~~


trembling frame as orchids his

time




additional-
ly is in center, forest existing
one—his

in the middle

~~

apprehension is only in front of its
motion by being
on it to the side
　　first where the hair-pin formation in one,
inchoate, and then dawn for instance.


~~


　　[and]


　　tendons hacked—fleeing camps.

　　in the middle—'on' one's
'his' dawn.

　　trees-fan walking

　　at night


~~

forest existing
his

a center—hurls—

[just]—[and] one's his-quiet

~~

the airs thin falls
'in' one—to be—close [to it]
    planks—people not caring for one
only—dread—at being
no moving away—in airs early
[captured in life—'as' dying]
    —as 'shape' of early—one's
—in 'his'-quiet's dawn also—
    no other activities—just one's

thin fans-rose forest existing only


~~


then—people speak the same—early
    —anticipating sounds—occur
before [them]—'in'

[captured in life 'in' dying—also—one's
    'his'-dawn

to] thin fans-rose forest now


~~

an elaborate darkness—the
    time span—she
    decides to ignore it

and brush on captured life—'in'
one
there
one does


~~

outer
fan—there isn't any
     —in it

captured in life in utter early
freedom
     and dying / others one
at all

and no outer fan
his

[his—[and]
fans-dawn 'there'—now]



~~




     not wanting to die ['as'] is present-time—
early thin fall high ['there'] has no base
     early thin fall day's-moon in high
'early' is ahead only
     walks—one's—trees-fan
on 'his' 'one's' early-present thin-forest existing
     'on' huge river—people
on mountains'-factories
     'his'-base walking on water, huge river—their
walking—night on mounds' carrying
     'his'-base walks

existing red trees-fans-base



~~

recent-past events—existing separate
sole
     as present ['in']—'is'
crowds crawling on black mounds
     singing—climbing—
one's walking on water 'there'
night—'his'-base walks thin

     in 'his' present early-'one'

     red trees-fan early-forest

     no time is necessary that's now—is it


~~


     his base walks
     one's—there's a space—in
between like throwing
—dawn's-trees-fan—is—early-instant's

space—this instant in
     the same
one—one's base walks—
     his-thin
moon's-day early


~~

    he will be outside
this instant's fall fans
    breath's alive at night 'his'
—'at' night
separately early—where—one's base walks


~~


are—their—rungs—there—breath's—?
'in'
night—'at' night
crawling lines on black mounds [coal] and
their climbing at night early—?

his quiet's—no moving away—captured in life


~~


    a switch

with flowers on it

    to take a switch

with flowers on it—night

additional-
    ly early


~~

—crowds surrounding before—to pull
the place down—they call in the army




    where
one walks on water—his quiet's-
    base—jump [one] in middle 'at'-dawn's
'there'
    'base's' middle 'yet'—[and]
—crowds surrounding—

    —on huge river—one's-dawn's
one jumps to or goes to [it]


~~


    —not—[captured in life]
[is conflict 'one'—why?]
    —in early
—walking
    one has a pair [is]
at present—'in'—'at'
    night's—[it]



~~

['it cannot be known']
falling—at night—in sky sleeping even—as one's
    present
base—space—'it can be known'—is
    [transgressing social
ridiculed for 'it can be known'—'in' [there being] 'no child'
    early child thinks
    then, right away—that was
accurate—dawn's at sky
    present
base-falling as fan's present striping away
    as transgressing 'even'

wide base-falling




~~


    their ridiculing at 'it can be known'
as eliminating—as—no base-falling
    'is'
one's-base-falling sky's 'even' action
    in night

wide


~~

as 'it can be known' being 'base-falling'—someone's
—so ridicule [a] one's-present
    'even'
transgressing
    into outside action—can't be known either

itself wide base-falling—['there']—in his-fan's-dawn
    'is' when transgressing itself 'there'
[as] additionally one's-black night


~~


    ridiculing—is the shell trick
—for social transgressing
    'is' no-social [transgresses] being [is] base-falling
one's
    no-base-falling night is fans—[neither]-occurs

so is present's 'at' night—[that's a base too,
    inaccurate


~~


    after ['as' occurrence] not being—black mounds
not being 'after' riding on moon
    as-action's quiet—it has none—hearing-moon—
existing
    isn't after occurring [moon's-hearing there]


~~

—to be brought into a
relation [social per se]—as being only dawn's-occurrence
 there [action]—one's
first is.—action is not a base

there is no base


~~


 no-night—were there no night—is
fans[-dawn]

 one's—there present-time
in 'it cannot be known'

 in early child—being
one's present-time not having to occur—
        'is'
 night—weighs


~~

one's




    fans-dawn in dusk only
—weighs it
    crowds
'it cannot be known'—space's—
    as tiny child right then
—is
               —there's
red—no trees



~~

removed—from one's basis
felt bereft, though its removing is that basis

    one

    we're in life with the mind always separate
from the mind
    feared 'captured in life' by dying
yet existing's existing too

~~

      to 'occur'
before
    there's its action [its occurrence]
isn't existing—is before its action then—'their'
    is one 'as' dawn's-action?—
there's action—and they're not—nights
not as a base 'one' or as their occurring—nights not being
    and which is before—throughout-is—before its-night

~~

      night's 'on'
humps—man's—lying beside him
     on huge water lying or walking—early
         —weighs—
'his-base' walking lying by one
     night's then on people on mounds' coal earlier


~~


       one's



     rain's red fall up—trees-
fans
             only—early
    trees walk
        'there' up


~~


    —breaths
—their—as no-volition—planks rung